TOP 50 Object Lessons

Games & Activities

Kathie R. Phillips

Plus
BONUS LESSONS
for Holidays, Popular Games, and **MORE!**

HENDRICKSON PUBLISHERS   ROSE KiDZ®

MW01093177

TOP 50 Object Lessons: Games & Activities
Copyright © 2017 Kathie R. Phillips

Rose Kidz® is an imprint of
Rose Publishing, LLC
P.O. Box 3473
Peabody, Massachusetts 01961-3473 USA
www.hendricksonrose.com\rosekidz
All rights reserved.

Cover and Interior Design by Nancy L. Haskins

ISBN: 978-1-62862-504-2
RoseKidz® reorder #R50009
RELIGION/Christian Ministry/Children

Printed in the United States of America
Printed July 2019

Table of Contents

BONUS LESSONS: GAMES

BONUS LESSONS: HOLIDAYS

BONUS LESSONS: CANDY

BONUS LESSONS: DISCOUNT STORE

Introduction

The Word of God is an amazing book, full of stories of men and women on journeys toward God and his love for them. These life-changing stories deserve to be told as creatively and enthusiastically as possible to help children grow closer to God and capture their imagination. Object lessons demonstrate and cement truth in their minds and help children focus on the truth you are trying to convey. Our best model for Object Lessons is Jesus. Jesus often used objects around him to teach truth. He took what was understood and familiar and connected it to a godly truth so that the truth would be more understood and familiar. Children learn the same way. Each of these lessons will do the same for the children you teach. Feel free to modify any of them to fit your needs and group size. In many cases, there are suggestions on low budget, small group alternatives. Please remember to ALWAYS inform parents before using any food or candy with their children.

> **Each lesson includes:**
> - Scripture
> - Easy-to-Do Prep
> - Discussion Questions
> - Supplies
> - Step-By-Step Instructions
> - Life Application
> - Additional Bible Stories each Object lesson can be used on
> - Easy to search Index in the back by: Topic, Type, and Bible Story

This resource may be used for weekly programs in your church or as supplemental material for Christian home educators.

FUN TYPES OF OBJECT LESSONS:

| Food | Kid-involved | Science | Everyday | Action | Messy | Games |

BONUS OBJECT LESSONS ON
· Games · Holidays · Candy · Dollar Store Items ·

It is my prayer that this resource helps children you influence personalize the messages of scripture for a lifetime impact.

Many Blessings,

Kathie Phillips

Object Lessons
TOP 50 TOPICS

Chapter 1: Bubbling Over

Scripture: "In your anger, do not sin": Do not let the sun go down while you are still angry."
– Ephesians 4:26, NIV

Purpose
To teach children that anger that stays bottled up can cause a big mess.

Type: Messy

Supplies:

- Small bottles of soda or carbonated water (8 ozs or 12 ozs)
- Index cards
- Pens/pencils/ markers

Preparation

Put index cards in groups of 10-12.

Tip:

If you think the children will not cooperate with the shaking of the bottle, you may want to just demonstrate this part yourself.

PRESENTATION

STEP 1: Divide the children into groups of 5-6.

SAY: There are many things that can make us mad, so mad sometimes, that we become angry. Make your best angry face for me right now. (*Give children the opportunity to make their best angry face.*) If I saw these faces, I would know for sure that you were angry! What are some other ways we know people are angry? (*Give children the opportunity to respond.*)
God gave us many emotions to feel. He, himself, experienced emotion. It's how we handle our emotions, however, that's important. Today, we're going to look at the emotion of anger and what happens when we let anger bottle up inside of us.

STEP 2: Hand each group a set of 10-12 index cards. In their groups, have them think of different scenarios that might make kids their age angry, i.e. moving to a new place, starting a different school, a sibling breaking a toy, being told 'no' by a parent, and write those scenarios on the index cards.

STEP 3: Collect the index cards from each

Take It Further

Connect this object lesson to other Bible passages:
- Cain and Abel (Genesis 4:1-16)
- Joseph and his brothers (Genesis 37)
- Sun go down on your anger (Ephesians 4:26)

group and invite one child from each group to come up front. Give each child a bottle of soda or carbonated water.

SAY: As I read one scenario from a card, decide how angry that scenario makes you on a scale of 1-10, with "1" being "cool as a cucumber" and "10" being "hot like fire". I want you to shake your soda bottle the same number you gave for your angry score. *(Read the cards)*

STEP 4: After the cards have been read, have the children return to their seats.

SAY: When some of our friends felt like a certain situation would make them angry, those soda bottles had lots of bubbles. After all of that shaking, what do you think would happen if I opened these soda bottles? *(Allow answers.)* That's right, we'd have a big mess on our hands. But that's what being angry and staying angry can do to us. It can cause a big mess.

STEP 5: Open one of the bottles and let it explode! Be sure to contain the mess.

SAY: That's why God doesn't want us to stay angry. Our anger can just blow up all over people. One of the ways we can release our anger is through prayer. Each time we pray to God some of our anger goes away. *(Release small amounts of the pressure in the bottle as you talk, eventually opening the bottle without an explosion.)* God wants us to turn to him for help when we are angry. We can go to him for relief.

DISCUSSION QUESTIONS

1. Have you ever been so angry that you thought you might explode? If so, tell us about that time.
2. What do you think are good ways to handle situations that might make us angry?
3. How can prayer help us calm down?

LIFE APPLICATION

SAY: There are many situations that make us angry, but our anger should not stay bottled up and cause us to sin. With God's help, we can handle those situations in ways that please him.

Wrap It Up

SAY: Many times in our life we will come across things that make us react in anger. When you feel that anger, your first response needs to be to ask God to help you control it. As we pray we release the pressure that builds up in us when we are angry.

Chapter 2: Deeply Rooted

Scripture: "...See to it that a bitter plant doesn't grow up. If it does, it will cause trouble. And it will pollute many people..." – Hebrews 12:15

Topic
Bitterness

Purpose
To help children understand how deep the roots of bitterness can go over time.

Type:
Everyday objects

Supplies:
- Picture of older tree (100+ years old)
- Baby plant in pot

Preparation
- Print up tree pictures
- Have baby plant on table up front

Tip
If you can take the class out to a large tree to finish the Object Lesson that will help them visualize how hard it would be to dig up the tree.

PRESENTATION

SAY: I want everyone to take a moment to think about a time someone hurt your feelings, made you feel bad about yourself, or bullied you. How did it make you feel? It may have caused you to be bitter. When we allow bitter feelings to stay in us they grow stronger and take a hold of us so it is harder to get over it.

STEP 1: Hold up the baby plant in the pot and the picture of the big tree.

SAY: Look at this baby plant and the picture of this really big tree. When someone first makes us upset and causes bitterness, it goes inside of us and takes hold, like the roots of this plant in the soil of this little pot. *(Hold up plant higher)* If we do nothing about it, these feelings stay and grow until they have roots in us as big as this tree. The roots on the little plant are not too far under the surface, but the older tree's roots go deep. *(Hold up picture of tree higher)* God wants us to be free of bitterness. He tells us

Take It Further
Connect this object lesson to other Bible passages:
- The Prodigal Son (Luke 15:11-32)
- Hannah prays for a son (1 Samuel 1:9-18)
- Get rid of all anger (Ephesians 4:31)

to forgive those that hurt us so we will be free and happier.

When we pray to God to forgive those who hurt us and truly want to remove that ugliness from our life, we pull that bitterness right out of us.

STEP 2: Pull up the plant out of the pot and expose the roots.

SAY: It is no longer in us. The roots of anger are removed from us.

STEP 3: Put down the plant and hold the picture of the tree up.

SAY: If we tried to dig up this older tree, how easy do you think that would be? *(Allow answers).* Digging up the older tree would be more difficult because its roots go way, way, deep. Bitterness is the same way. If we allow bitterness to take root in our hearts, it can go down deep and be much harder to get rid of.

DISCUSSION QUESTIONS

1. Why do you think the roots of bitterness can go deep beneath the surface?

2. What are some things that cause you to be bitter?

3. What should you do to get rid of bitterness?

LIFE APPLICATION

SAY: People of all ages can struggle with unhappy feelings, even kids your age. How often do you say or think, "That's not fair!" Maybe someone you feel who is undeserving won a prize or a place on a sports team. Maybe your brother or sister was rewarded for good behavior unfairly. Although something might seem unfair at the moment, God doesn't want those feelings to cause us to turn into bitterness.

Wrap It Up

SAY: When you feel angry, immediately pray and ask God to help you get over your anger. There may a good reason to be angry. It may cause you to make something right, but staying angry only hurts you. Ask God to do what is needed and let the anger go.

Chapter 3: Loosen Your Grip

Scripture: "In your heart you plan your life. But the Lord decides where your steps will take you."
— Proverbs 16:9

Topic
Control

Purpose
To help children understand that God is ultimately in control.

Type:
Kid Volunteer

Supplies:
- TV remote

Preparation
Pick a child you know will work with you up front. Have him pretend you have a remote that controls their actions. When you say, " I have a remote that controls one of you," stand up when you see me push a button. Then you will say what button you are pushing so they know how to act. Tell him/her to do whatever you say the button does.

PRESENTATION

STEP 1: Stand up front with a remote control in your hand.

SAY: Today I want to show you an amazing remote control. It is programmed to control one of you. *(push the button)* Oh, it is a (Tommy remote). Let's see what kind of control I have over him. Let me push the hop button. *(Push a bottom and have him/her hop).* Wow, I can have him/her do whatever I want. That is a lot of power and control. Would you want me to have a remote that controls you? *(Allow answers, thank (Tommy) and have him take a seat, using the remote).*

The truth is, most people don't really like being told what to do. We like having the freedom to do what we want when we want it. We like to be in charge and in control. We like to think we are the boss. The Bible, however, says different.

STEP 2: Read Proverbs 16:9 aloud.

SAY: God tells us that it is okay to plan out what we want to do, but he wants to be directing our steps. He knows what is best for us. He wants us to know when things happen, he is directing it to allow good

Take It Further

Connect this object lesson to other Bible passages:
- Pharaoh's edict (Exodus 1)
- King Nebuchadnezzar (Daniel 1-6)
- King Herod (Matthew 2:13-18)

in our life. We have to stay in this. *(Hold up the Bible)* We need to come to church and hear what he wants to tell us. When we listen, he lets us know what plans are best to choose. We work together with him to plan. When we try to figure out things on our own and don't listen to God, things go wrong.

Instead of trying to be in control of things and people, our goal should be to follow God's lead. He is the one in control and knows what's best. He wants to be in control of the plans you make, the words you say, the things you do, and the places you go. Why? Because he wants what is best for you.

STEP 3: Hold up the Bible.

SAY: The Bible tells us that God has a plan for us. He decides where our steps will take us. It is a good plan that will give us hope and a bright future, but we will never see that plan work unless we allow God to be in control. So what can we do? Learn what God wants us to do by reading the Bible and talking to him.

DISCUSSION QUESTIONS

1. Is it hard for you to not be in control?

2. Why might that be easy? Why might that be hard?

3. Does knowing God is in ultimate control help you in tough situations?

LIFE APPLICATION

SAY: Children your age face many tough situations. No matter what difficulties you face, you can trust God. He knows and loves you and is in control of all things. We can trust God no matter what. All we have to do is give him the control of our choices.

Wrap It Up

SAY: We need to stay close to God. We need to read the Bible and pray. Expect that God will guide you as you go through life. If you don't, you are setting yourself up to have tough times.

Chapter 4: Marble-lous

Scripture: "Be strong and courageous."
–Deuteronomy 31:6, NIV

Topic
Courage

Purpose

To help children see that with God's help, they can be courageous.

Type:
Food
Kid Volunteer

Supplies:

- Marbles
- Bowls filled with the following items: prepared chocolate pudding, cooked spaghetti, prepared gelatin
- Brown paper lunch bags
- Clear plastic container
- Wipes to clean hands

Preparation

Place each item in an individual bowl and hide a marble in each bowl. Then place the bowls inside of the brown lunch bags. Place the remaining marbles in a clear plastic container.
Set the bags and the jar of marbles on a table in front of the children.

PRESENTATION

SAY: When I was younger, I loved to play with marbles.

STEP 1: Hold up the marbles.

> **SAY:** Do any of you like to play with marbles? *(Allow answers.)* There are many cool things you can do with marbles. Since I have so many marbles at home, I'd like to give these marbles away. Who would like to have these marbles that I brought in? *(Allow answers)*

STEP 2: Invite a child to come up to the table and give them the jar of marbles.

> **SAY:** Oh no! This jar of marbles feels a little light. I think some are missing. That's right…some are in these brown paper bags. *[Name of volunteer]*, will you dig them out of these bags. Just so you know there is something else in there with them. Do you have enough courage to dig in these bags to find the missing marbles? *(Allow answers.)*

Take It Further

Connect this object lesson to other Bible passages:

- Esther (Esther 3-8)
- David and Goliath (1 Samuel 17)
- Rahab and the Spies (Joshua 2)

 Top 50 Object Lessons: Games & Activities

Object Lesson:
Courage

STEP 3: One at a time, have him/her dig into the bowls in the bags to retrieve the missing marbles. After all of the marbles have been retrieved, provide them with a hand wipe to clean their hands and give them the jar of marbles to take home.

SAY: [Name of child] showed a great deal of courage today! Sticking your hand into a bag of unknown items is a bit scary. A lot of us face scary times. We need God to give us strength and courage to help us.

STEP 4: Read Deuteronomy 31:6.

SAY: This verse tells us that God gives us strength when we need it. He is with us when we're scared or afraid. Praying helps us call on God to help us when we are afraid. When we don't know what will happen (when we stick our hand in a bag). We can talk to God and trust that he will help us be strong and courageous.

? DISCUSSION QUESTIONS

1. What makes you have courage in scary or unknown situations?
2. What promises from God's Word can you remember?
3. Have you ever asked God to help you when you were scared? What happened?

LIFE APPLICATION

SAY: Children just like you can have many fears – fear of the dark, fear of new situations, fear of getting hurt. With God's help, you can be strong and courageous because he is with you.

Wrap It Up

SAY: When you are feeling afraid, stop and pray. God hears you and already knows you are afraid. He is right there waiting for you to invite him into your life to help you in tough times.

Chapter 5: Fair, Not Fair

Scripture: *"...I have learned to be content no matter what happens to me. – Philippians 4:11*

Topic
Discontent

Purpose

To help children understand being content with what they have.

Type:
Kid volunteer

Supplies:

- 1 penny
- 1 dime
- 1 quarter

Preparation

Make a list of questions that each child is guaranteed to correctly answer.

PRESENTATION

STEP 1: Call up 3 children to answer a series of questions. Each child will answer an easy question and be rewarded a point. At the end of the round, tally the points (the children should all have the same amount). Reward the children as follows:

- 1 child will be rewarded a quarter
- 1 child will be rewarded a dime
- 1 child will be rewarded a penny

By this time, they (or the other children in the room) might be expressing unfairness or displeasure at the rewards two of the children received. If this occurs, act oblivious.

SAY: What? Those rewards aren't fair? Why not? *(Allow answers)* If I hear you correctly, you are telling me that it isn't fair two of my volunteers received less than one child, even though everyone had the same amount of points. Is that correct? *(Allow answers)* So you think that everyone should have received the same reward. I think I even heard some of you say, "That's not fair."

Take It Further

Connect this object lesson to other Bible passages:

- Prodigal Son (Luke 15:11-32)
- Mary and Martha (Luke 10:38-42)
- Love of money (1 Timothy 6:6-8)

 Top 50 Object Lessons: Games & Activities

STEP 2: Turn to the participants and ask:

SAY: How did it feel to receive the prize you did, even though everyone had the same amount of points?

STEP 3: After the participants have responded, thank them and instruct them to take a seat.

SAY: Have you ever experienced feelings of joy and then jealousy soon after? *(Allow answers)* I think many of us have. Sometimes we look at what others have and think it's not fair when we don't have those things, even when we feel like we deserve it. There is nothing wrong with admiring things other people have. The problem comes when we want what someone else has so much that it makes us not appreciate what we have. Imagine taking a gift to a friend's birthday party and your friend loves someone else's gift more than the gift you gave. That might be how God feels when we feel like what he's given is not enough. The apostle Paul taught about this.

STEP 4: Read Philippians 4:11.

SAY: No matter what happened to Paul, he had decided to be content. What about you? Are you content no matter what you have?

DISCUSSION QUESTIONS

1. Have you ever felt that someone had better things than you?
2. Why do you think you felt that way?
3. What can you do to be more content with what you have?

LIFE APPLICATION

SAY: There are many, many flashy new toys, gadgets, and clothes that are available to you. Sometimes, the way you think of yourself is based on what you have (or don't have). Having a lot of things doesn't make you better or less than anyone. You can be satisfied with what they already have because you are enough.

Wrap It Up

SAY: We need to be thankful for what we do have and not want what everyone else has. Learn this verse and ask God to help you be content and grateful.

Chapter 6: Follow the Leader

Scripture: *"My sheep listen to my voice; I know them, and they follow me."* – John 10:27, NIV

Topic
Disobedience

Purpose
To help children understand that disobedience is a choice that can have consequences.

Type:
Action

Supplies:
- 1 traffic cone /or anything that marks a boundary
- 1 large flag

Preparation

Have all of the children stand up and move to one end of the room. On the opposite side of the room, place the cone on the floor and attach the flag to it. (This area will be the goal.)

PRESENTATION

STEP 1: Explain to the children that you will give them a series of commands that will lead them to the flag and cone. However, they should do the opposite of the commands you give. (For example, they will go left if you say to go right.) Begin the game and play for a few minutes or until a child reaches the goal.

STEP 2: Have the kids sit back down.

SAY: That game was pretty simple, but it was also complicated. It was simple because there was a goal in front of you, but it was complicated because getting to the goal took some extra effort from you. I told you one thing, but you had to do the opposite. For some of you, it was hard to remember what exactly you were doing!

Making the choice to obey is very similar. Someone who loves and cares for us, like God, your parents, or teachers, tells you to do something and you have a choice – to do what they say or to do the opposite. If you

TAKE IT FURTHER

Connect this object lesson to other Bible passages:
- The Ten Commandments (Exodus 20)
- Samson (Judges 13-16)
- Jonah to Nineveh (Jonah 1)

Object Lesson: Disobedience

do the opposite, you are disobeying. Just like our game showed, when we choose to do the opposite of the person guiding us, we can get confused. There might even be a consequence like getting lost or getting hurt.

STEP 3: Hold up your Bible and read John 10:27.

SAY: Who do you think is speaking in this verse? *(Allow answers.)* Jesus, the Shepherd, says his sheep know him and follow him. That is obedience. Jesus wants us to follow him and other adults who lead us. When we follow God we are obeying and can be closer to God.

What do you think would happen if the sheep didn't follow the shepherd? *(Allow answers)* They could end up in danger, alone, hungry, or lost. God wants us to be in his care. He sees what is coming and knows how to prepare you for it. Sometimes it may seem like a bad thing is happening and God is not in control, but God knows that sometimes we have to go through a bad thing with him to learn how to handle a worse thing down the road. Trust him, follow him and he will take care of you.

DISCUSSION QUESTIONS

1. Is it hard for you to obey those in charge?

2. Why is that hard?

3. Why do you think it's important to be obedient?

LIFE APPLICATION

SAY: Following someone's lead can be hard, but it's for our benefit to trust those God puts in leadership over us. Our Christian walk is a life of obeying God first, and then others he puts in our lives.

Wrap It Up

SAY: When we follow God and those he gives to teach and guide us, we are telling God that we trust him and want him to be in control of our lives. Our lives will be better because of it.

Chapter 7: Got Faith?

Scripture: *"Now faith is confidence in what we hope for and assurance about what we do not see."*
– Hebrews 11:1, NIV

Topic
Faith

Purpose
To help children understand that they can have faith in God even if they can't see him.

Type:
Kid volunteer

Supplies:

- 1 blindfold
- Toy hoop
- Red, yellow and/or orange streamers
- Tape

Preparation

Use the tape to attach 6-inch pieces of the streamers to the toy hoop. Keep out of sight of the children until noted.

PRESENTATION

STEP 1: Invite a child to come up to the front of the group.

> **SAY:** How much do you trust me? *(Allow answers.)* How much would you trust me if I blindfolded you and had you stand in front of the group? *(Allow answers, then blindfold the child.)*

STEP 2: With the child blindfolded ask.

> **SAY:** Have you ever been to the circus? Well today I want you to practice one of my favorite circus acts – the ring of fire. I want you to walk through this ring of fire. *(Bring out the toy hoop, but look at the rest of the kids and motion for them to not give it away.)* As you walk through the ring of fire I want you to know that you can trust me that you will not be burned.

STEP 3: Excite the remaining children by getting them to cheer on the blindfolded child. With your help, guide the blindfolded child to step

Take It Further

Connect this object lesson to other Bible passages:

- Abraham and Isaac (Genesis 22:1-14)
- Mary and the Angel (Luke 1:26-38)
- Hebrews faith "Hall of Fame" (Hebrews 11)

Object Lesson: Faith

through the hoop. Take the blindfold off of the child and have him/her see the 'ring of fire.'

SAY: Thank you for participating. *(Have him/her be seated.)*
There are many things we know for sure and many things we don't. Trusting in things we don't know or can't see requires faith. My friend *[name of blindfolded child]* trusted me to guide him/her through what they thought was a ring of fire. He/she trusted me to keep him safe.

STEP 4: Read Hebrews 11:1.

SAY: Having faith in God is like that. We can't see God, but we trust in him to be there for us and to help us when we don't know how things will turn out. Having faith in God means trusting him to work it all out.

DISCUSSION QUESTIONS

1. When have you had to have faith in God?

2. Was it easy or hard?

3. What are you trusting God for right now?

LIFE APPLICATION

SAY: Being a follower of Jesus involves a lot of faith. We can't see him, but if we have faith in God's Word, we know that he's always with us, always loves us, and always keeps his promises.

Wrap It Up

SAY: Isn't it great that we can trust God to take good care of us? When we have faith in him, we have the courage to step into things that are scary or unknown knowing he will go with us.

Chapter 8: Family Ties

Scripture: "Choose for yourselves this day whom you will serve ... but as for me and my household, we will serve the LORD." – Joshua 24:15, NIV

Topic
Family

Purpose
To help children realize the importance of family in their lives.

Type:
Everyday objects

Supplies:
- A bicycle tire with spokes

Preparation
Have the bicycle tire on stage with you.

PRESENTATION

SAY: I want to talk to you a bit today about family. What do I have here?

STEP 1: Hold up the tire.

SAY: That's right, I have a bicycle tire. Now what is interesting about this tire is that is a great example of our families. The first thing I want to look at is the hub in the middle. *(Point to the mechanism in the center.)* This hub represents God. Where is that hub located in this family wheel? *(Allow answers)* That's right, at the center. If this hub was not at the center, the wheel would be out of alignment and wobble all over. *(Motion the wheel in a crazy way.)*

It is important for everything to run smoothly, that the hub is at the center. Just like us it is important for us to keep God at the center of all our families do.

STEP 2: Point to the spokes.

SAY: Then we have the spokes. We can see that as each spoke is connected

Take It Further

Connect this object lesson to other Bible passages:
- Joseph and his brothers (Genesis 37)
- Jacob and Esau (Genesis 25:19-34)
- Ruth and Naomi (Ruth 1)

to the hub and goes out, it is lined up, strong and connected. If a spoke disconnects from the hub, the tire will wobble and become unstable. We each have a responsibility to stay close to God to help our family stay strong.

STEP 3: Move your finger along the spoke from outside to the center and then from the center to the outside.

SAY: Also, see how the spokes, as they draw closer to the hub they draw closer to each other, and as they move away from the hub they move away from each other?

That is how it is with our families. As we each draw close to God it causes us to draw closer to each other. It also makes us stronger. Do all you can to stay close to God and each other. Keep him at the center of your family.

DISCUSSION QUESTIONS

1. What is one good thing about being in your family?

2. How can you help each other stay close to God?

3. How can you love your family well this week?

LIFE APPLICATION

SAY: Our family members are not always easy to get along with, but when God is at the center of our families, we can live at peace with everyone. Families love us and support us. They give us a place to belong. You are a very important part of your family and God's family.

Wrap It Up

SAY: Be aware that as you are growing closer to God you are also helping your family grow closer to each other and God. Do your part to help the family stay close to God.

Chapter 9: Fear Factor

Scripture: "I can do all this through him who gives me strength." – Philippians 4:13, NIV

Topic
Fear

Purpose
To remind children that they do not have to be consumed by fear.

Type:
Kid Volunteer

Supplies:

- Blue sheets of construction paper
- 4 envelopes
- 4 index cards
- Black marker
- Toy spiders and toy rubber snake
- Rope (at least 3')

Preparation

With marker write "WATER" on each sheet. Write 'Challenge Envelope' on 4 envelopes. Place 1 index card with 1 of the four challenges on it.
- WALK ON WATER
- BE COVERED IN SPIDERS
- HOLD A SNAKE
- WALK A TIGHTROPE
Place remaining supplies close by and out of sight.

PRESENTATION

SAY: Sometimes, I like to challenge myself. *(Share an appropriate story of setting a challenge with the children.)* Maybe you've challenged yourself before. Maybe you've challenged yourself to memorize a Bible verse or read 10 books this year. Some people like challenges and some people don't. Some challenges are easy and some take courage because they're a little hard or scary. Having courage means doing something that might be unknown or scary. I need 4 volunteers to come up and help me.

STEP 1: Choose 4 children to come up to the front. Give each child a "Challenge Envelope." Once all of the envelopes have been distributed, have the children open their envelopes.

> **SAY:** *(Starting with first child)* Read your card aloud to the group. *(Have them read it.)* Are you ready to accomplish this challenge?

STEP 2-5: Follow the direction for each challenge as they come up in the cards.
> **Challenge 1:** WALK ON WATER -

Take It Further

Connect this object lesson to other Bible passages:
- Mary and the angel (Luke 1:26-38)
- Daniel in the Lions' Den (Daniel 6)
- Jesus calms the storm (Mark 4:35-41)

Object Lesson: Fear

Spread the sheets of construction paper out on the floor and have the child walk on them.

> **Challenge 2:** BE COVERED WITH SPIDERS - Pour the toy spiders over the child.
> **Challenge 3:** HOLD A SNAKE - Have the child hold the toy snake.
> **Challenge 4:** WALK ON A TIGHTROPE- Have the child walk on a rope that is laid on the ground.

SAY: How much courage did it take to do the challenge before you knew what was going to really happen? *(Allow answers.)* What was going through your head? *(Thank them for being courageous and have them return to their seats.)*

How many of you were afraid for your friends when you heard the challenges they would be facing? *(Allow answers.)* God's Word, the Bible, gives us courage when we face scary situations.

STEP 6: Read Philippians 4:13 aloud.

SAY: Just reading that makes me feel braver.

DISCUSSION QUESTIONS

1. What are some things that children your age are afraid of?

2. What helps you when you might be afraid?

LIFE APPLICATION

SAY: We all face scary times, but God's promises from the Bible gives us strength to be brave. When we talk to God in prayer, he gives us courage when we are afraid. Trust in God to give you the strength you need to face whatever comes your way.

Wrap It Up

SAY: Remember when you are afraid to pray. Spend time learning the Bible so when you are faced with challenges and scary situations, God can remind you of his promises so you can be brave and courageous.

Chapter 10: Restoration

Scripture: "Those who erase a sin by forgiving it show love." – Proverbs 17:9

Topic
Forgiveness

Purpose
To show children that relationships can be restored with forgiveness.

Type:
Everyday objects

Supplies:
- 1 old penny
- Pencil with erasers

Preparation
Set out the pennies and eraser on a hard surface, like a table. Practice this ahead of time to figure timing and effectiveness.

Tip
Use the type of erasers that fit down over the top of a pencil eraser. This will help it get into the recessed parts of the penny.

PRESENTATION

SAY: Do you own anything really special, so special that you don't want anyone to touch? Sometimes, we own something that's so special to us that we do all we can to protect it to keep from getting lost or broken. Think about the people you know and love. I bet they're pretty special to you. The relationships we have with people we're close to are even more special than that special item you don't want anyone to touch. If we're not careful, relationships can be broken and need fixing.

Sometimes, feelings get hurt when you fight with a family member or friend. Sometimes, there are misunderstandings about things that can make people not want to spend time together anymore. Our relationships get ugly.

STEP 1: Hold up the dirty penny.

SAY: Our relationship can look like this ugly penny. However, it's not healthy to leave those relationships broken. You have to do your part to fix them by forgiving, even when it's hard.

Look at this penny. *(Hold up the penny.)*

Take It Further

Connect this object lesson to other Bible passages:
- Joseph and his brothers (Genesis 50:15-21)
- Jesus forgives the criminal (Luke 23:32-43)
- Jesus forgives and heals a paralyzed man (Mark 2:1-12)

 Top 50 Object Lessons: Games & Activities

It looks old and worn. Let's pretend this eraser is forgiveness. With a little time, love, and effort on our part we can restore our relationships to people we care about to as good as new.

STEP 2: Read Proverbs 17:9.

  SAY: What does this verse tell you about forgiveness? It says we have to do something. It will not just happen that your relationships get cleaned up. You have to forgive.

STEP 3: Use the eraser to clean the penny until they shine. Hold up the shiny penny.

  SAY: Now I needed to work at that. It took some effort on my part. It didn't clean up fast. When we forgive we show God's love and invite God into the situation to help heal it.

DISCUSSION QUESTIONS

1. When have you had to forgive someone who's wronged you?

2. Have you ever had to ask for someone to forgive you?

3. Which was easier for you?

LIFE APPLICATION

SAY: There are many situations that make us angry, but our anger should not stay bottled up and cause us to sin. With God's help, we can handle those situations in ways that please him.

Wrap It Up

SAY: When you forgive someone who has wronged you, the relationship with that person can be restored. It might be hard but it will be worth it!

Chapter 11: **Stuck Together**

Scripture: *"A friend loves at all times."*
– Proverbs 17:17

Topic
Friendship

Purpose
To illustrate how good friends stick together.

Type:
Food
Kid volunteer

Supplies:
- Toothpicks
- Marshmallows

Preparation

Decide in advance how to divide the children into groups. Set up stations with marshmallows and toothpicks.

PRESENTATION

STEP 1: Divide the children into groups.

SAY: Today we are going to see how we can support each other. We are going to have a contest to see which group can build the biggest tower. You can only use what is in front of you.

STEP 2: After a few minutes call time and see who has the best tower that can stand on its own.

SAY: We can see that when we stick together we are stronger and can accomplish more. Friends make life fun! When we pick friends that love God too, we can help each other do the right things. What would happen if one of our friends was not doing the right thing? What if I melted one of these marshmallows? *(Allow answers)* That's right, our entire tower would fall. It is important to hang around with friends

Take It Further

Connect this object lesson to other Bible passages:
- David and Jonathan (1 Samuel 20)
- Peter and Jesus (Matthew 26:31-35)
- A friend loves at all times (Proverbs 17:17)

that do the right thing. You should also remember that it is important for you to stay close to God and do the right things to be a strong support to your friends too.

STEP 3: Read Proverbs 17:17.

SAY: This verse reminds us that when we have friends that love each other and stick together through the good and the bad, we are stronger together.

DISCUSSION QUESTIONS

1. What kinds of things do you like to do with your friends?
2. Do you have friends that love God?
3. Do your Christian friends help you make good choices?

LIFE APPLICATION

SAY: God gives us friends to help and love us. He wants us to choose our friends wisely so that our friendships are good and strong. Good friends stick together through happy times as well as sad times so that we don't have to be alone.

Wrap It Up

SAY: Choosing good friends helps us. We are stronger when we have others to go through the ups and downs of life with.

Chapter 12: Cheerful Giver

Scripture: *"God loves a cheerful giver."*
–2 Corinthians 9:7

Topic
Giving/ Generosity

Type:
Everyday objects

Supplies:
- Basket of books
- Newspaper

Preparation

None

Purpose
To help children understand that God wants them to give cheerfully.

PRESENTATION

STEP 1: Walk up to the front of the group with your basket of books.

SAY: Can you tell that I love to read? I was doing some cleaning and realized that I have so many books. Does anyone here love to read? *(Allow answers.)* In fact, I have so many books that I have run out of room on my bookshelf. I wonder what I could do with the ones I don't need anymore. *(Look as if you are thinking.)*

STEP 2: Pick up newspaper and begin to read the following:

SAY: "Local shelter looking for new or gently-used books for its residents."

Aha! That's it! I can give away some of my books to help others. *(Start to choose books from the basket to give away and then hesitate.)* Wait a minute...this is one of my favorite books. *(Clutch books to your chest.)* I can't give this one away. *(Set that book*

Take It Further

Connect this object lesson to other Bible passages:
- Jesus Feeds 5000 (Matthew 14:13-21)
- Woman washes Jesus' feet (Luke 7:36-50)
- The Good Samaritan (Luke 10:25-37)

to the side. Then look through the basket and choose a few more to set aside as your favorites.)

Oh no! I can't give these books away...or can I? I mean, I don't read them anymore and I'm running out of space on my bookshelf. *(Pick up newspaper and read it again.)* "Local shelter looking for new or gently-used books for its residents."

Even though these books are my favorites and I'll miss them dearly, I think it's time for me to bless someone else who could use them more than I can. That's what I'll do!

STEP 3: Read Proverbs 17:17.

SAY: It isn't enough for us to give to God our time, money and talents. He wants us to do it happily. If I was upset about giving away these books, it would still be a blessing to whomever got them, but I would miss out on the great feelings God wants to share with me for giving them with a happy spirit.

DISCUSSION QUESTIONS

1. Why do you think God wants us to be cheerful when giving?

2. Do you think our attitude affects how we give?

3. What can you give to bless someone else?

LIFE APPLICATION

SAY: Many of us have so much more than we really need that we can bless others through our abundance. God doesn't want us to have so much extra when we bless someone who doesn't have as much as we do. He wants to give out of our abundance and do so with a cheerful heart.

Wrap It Up

SAY: The next time you give to God, whether it be money, or time, or things, do it with a happy spirit. God will bless you and others because of it.

Chapter 13: God Goals

Scripture: "Commit to the LORD everything you do. Then your plans will succeed."

– Proverbs 16:3

Topic
Goals

Purpose
To guide children in seeing where God fits into their plans.

Type:
Everyday objects

Supplies:
- Easel or whiteboard
- Markers
- Easel pad (if using easel)

Preparation
Write a checklist of 3 goals on the easel pad or whiteboard.

PRESENTATION

STEP 1: Have the easel next to you.

SAY: Every January 1, many people make resolutions (or goals) for the new year. Here are 3 of my goals. *(Show goals written on easel pad or whiteboard.)*

Setting goals helps keep us on track to make things happen. Without goals, we don't have anything to work toward.

STEP 2: Read Proverbs 16:3.

SAY: This verse reminds us that although we may have plans, God is the one ultimately in control of those plans. Since he is in control, it would be wise to seek him and pray for wisdom in setting our goals.

STEP 3: Look at the list on the easel pad or whiteboard.

SAY: I wonder what God would

Take It Further

Connect this object lesson to other Bible passages:
- Finish the race Acts 20:23-24
- He will make your plans succeed Proverbs 16:3
- Goal to win the prize Philippians 3:14-15

want me to do with this list. I'll pray and ask him to help me decide if these are goals I should have. Who thinks I should have prayed and asked God to help me make the goals before I decided on them? *(Allow answers)*

That's right, we should first ask God to guide us before we make decision. What decisions do you need to make? Should we only be thinking about this on January 1st? *(Allow answers)* That's right, we make decisions every day, all day long. In the morning before you start your day, you need to begin with praying and asking God to guide your steps and help you move on his path. He will help you see the right way to go.

DISCUSSION QUESTIONS

1. What goals are you working toward?

2. Have you asked God to help you have the right goals?

3. Who can help you reach your goals?

LIFE APPLICATION

SAY: It's easy to think that you don't need God's help with things you want to do. You know what you want to do and you do them. What might change if you ask God to tell you what he wants you to do before you make a plan? How might the plan look different?

Wrap It Up

SAY: It is comforting to know that God cares so much about you that he wants to be involved in what happens to you throughout the day. When we take time to check with God on decisions, he will help us make the right choices.

Chapter 14: Never Ending

Scripture: "...I have loved you with a love that lasts forever. I have kept on loving you with faithful love."
– Jeremiah 31:3

Topic
God's love for me

Purpose
To help children discover the depth of God's love for them.

Type:
Kid volunteer

Supplies:
- Toy Hoops

Preparation
None.

PRESENTATION

SAY: How many of you like to toy hoop? *(Allow kids to respond.)*

STEP 1: Invite a few to come up front and use the hoops. After a minute or two, have the children stop and hold the toy hoop in place.

SAY: I wonder if I could give you another challenge. I challenge you to find the beginning of this circle. *(Allow the kids to try to find the starting point of their toy hoop.)*

Circles are pretty cool shapes. They have no beginning and no end. God's love for us is the same way; it has no beginning and no end. No matter who we are, what we've done or what we're going to do, God's love for us will stay the same. *(Have the kids sit down.)*

STEP 2: Read Jeremiah 31:3.

SAY: God's love for you *(point to*

Take It Further

Connect this object lesson to other Bible passages:
- Called children of God 1 John 3:1
- How wide, long, high, and deep Ephesians 3:18
- Christ died for us. Romans 5:8

a child, and then another and then another each time repeating "and you") and all of you, never, ever stops and it never, ever fails. Imagine that with me for a moment. God knows who you are, everything about you. All the good things you are and things you do and all the bad things you do, even your thoughts, and **he loves you! FOREVER! FOREVER!** How amazing is that? Just like this circle of the toy hoop. It just keeps going on. *(Move your hand around and around the circle.)* That is the best news of all!

DISCUSSION QUESTIONS

1. What does it feel to know that God loves you?

2. Have you accepted the unending love God has for you?

LIFE APPLICATION

SAY: Nothing you have done and nothing you will ever do will make God's love for you change. He will never stop loving you. He loved you so much that giving his greatest gift of love, his only son, Jesus, means that you can live with God forever. All you have to do is accept the gift.

Wrap It Up

SAY: Whenever we see a circle that has no beginning or end, like a ring or a hoop, we can be reminded of the love God has for us.

Chapter 15: Heart of Thankfulness

Scripture: "Give thanks in all circumstances; for this is God's will for you in Christ Jesus."

– 1 Thessalonians 5:18, NIV

Topic
Gratitude

Purpose
To illustrate just how full a heart filled with thankfulness can be.

Type:
Everyday objects

Supplies:
- 2 Heart-shaped balloons
- Marker

Preparation
Blow up the first balloon and tie it off. Place this up front with a permanent marker. Inflate the second balloon, but do not tie it. Once the balloon is inflated, use the marker to write the word "Thankful" on it. Then deflate the balloon.

Tip
This object lesson runs better if you have a helper.

PRESENTATION

SAY: I love Thanksgiving! It's my favorite holiday. I love it because it's a day that we set aside to reflect on all of our blessings! We have so much to be thankful for. The special thing is that we don't need to save up our thankfulness and gratefulness for just one day of the year. Every day can be Thanksgiving!

STEP 1: Read 1 Thessalonians 5:18.

> **SAY:** Let's work together to create a heart of thankfulness. Think of one thing you are grateful for and raise your hand. *(Write their answers on the first, tied o˜ balloon.)*

STEP 2: As you call on them to share what they're thankful for, have an assistant add a puff of air to inflate the second heart-shaped balloon. *(Or you could multi-task if necessary)*

Take It Further

Connect this object lesson to other Bible passages:
- Every good and perfect gift (James 1:17)
- The Lord looks at what is in the heart (1 Samuel 16:7)
- David praises God (Psalm 138)

SAY: Wow, our balloon is getting full of thankfulness. We may need to be careful or it may pop.

STEP 3: After everyone has shared, tie off the balloon.

SAY: When we count our blessings, our hearts fill with thankfulness. The more blessings we count, the bigger our hearts grow. God wants us to have a heart filled to overflowing with thanksgiving for all he's given us!

DISCUSSION QUESTIONS

1. What are you grateful for?

2. Do you express your gratefulness often?

3. How can counting your blessings become part of your everyday life?

LIFE APPLICATION

SAY: As we intentionally think about what we are thankful for, our heart learns to be more and more thankful. A thankful heart also recognizes that every blessing we have comes from God. Don't take for granted the many ways God has blessed you!

Wrap It Up

SAY: Make an effort to think of all the good things God has done for you and all the blessings he has given you. When you feel yourself focusing on something bad, change the direction of your thinking and remember what you are thankful for.

Chapter 16: More Than Meets the Eye

Scripture: "Don't you know that your bodies are temples of the Holy Spirit?"   – 1 Corinthians 6:19

Topic
Health

Type:
Everyday objects

Supplies:

- Rotating cube puzzle
- Jump rope
- Stress ball
- Party hat
- Noisemaker
- Confetti (optional)

Preparation

None.

Purpose
To help kids understand that being healthy is more than just physical.

PRESENTATION

SAY: Raise your hand if you have ever heard the following at your house:
1. "Exercise your brain."
2. "Eat your fruits and vegetables."
3. "Calm down!"
4. "Do you want to invite a friend over to hang out?"

I'm pretty sure you have or something like it. The grown-ups in your lives tell you these things not to bug you, but to help you be healthy. Being healthy means being more than physically healthy (which is good), but they want you to be healthy inside AND out.

STEP 1: Read 1 Corinthians 6:19.

SAY: What does a temple of God mean? *(Allow answers)* If Jesus lives in our heart then we are actually a holy place. We need to respect our bodies just like we respect church. Let's look deeper at this.

STEP 2: Hold up and manipulate the rotating cube puzzle.

SAY: This little cube can help you stay mentally healthy. It'll give your brain a good workout and help you to problem-solve. When we learn school work, read, or memorize scripture we are exercising our brain.

Take It Further

Connect this object lesson to other Bible passages:
- Daniel eats vegetables (Daniel 1)
- Goal to win the prize (Philippians 3:14)
- A peaceful heart (Proverbs 14:30)

STEP 3: Hold up the jump rope and jump.

SAY: Physical activities like jumping rope help you to get your heart rate up and have a healthy body. God wants us to take good care of our body by exercising, playing sports, eating well, and getting enough sleep.

STEP 4: Hold up and manipulate the stress ball.

SAY: Sometimes, you are faced with situations that make you angry, frustrated, or confused. Staying healthy in this way means finding good ways to help you handle those difficult situations. Some people squeeze a stress ball to calm down. I like to pray. God helps me calm down. I know when I pray I am inviting God to help me solve the problem I am stressed about.

Another way to be healthy is to make time for fun! Spending time with family and friends can make your heart glad. So, put on your party hat *(put on the party hat)* and have a party! *(Blow the noisemaker and toss the confetti.)*

When we treat our body like a holy temple of God we are living the way God intended us to.

DISCUSSION QUESTIONS

1. Is staying healthy important to you?

2. How do you stay healthy?

3. What is one thing you can do to be even more healthy?

LIFE APPLICATION

SAY: So many activities can keep you a very busy kid! Being healthy mentally, physically, emotionally, and socially will go a long way in helping you be the healthiest kid you can be!

Wrap It Up

SAY: We are told we are a holy temple of God. It is our job to make choices that keep us healthy. Take time to make good choices.

Chapter 17: Untangled

Scripture: *"...let us throw off everything that hinders and the sin that so easily entangles..."*
– Hebrews 12:1, NIV

Topic
Honesty

Purpose
To illustrate that a web of lies can spin out of control.

Type:
Kid Volunteer
Everyday object

Supplies:
- Yarn
- Scissors

Preparation
Talk with a child ahead of time about helping you up front.

PRESENTATION

STEP 1: Invite the child you talked to up front. Hand him/her one end of the yarn.

SAY: Who here has told a lie? *(show of hands)* Look at your volunteer and ask the same question. *(If they say no, wrap them in one circle of yarn.)* What are some lies that maybe some of you have heard or told? *(After every suggestion, wrap up the child in yarn.)* Maybe you lied about mistreating your brother or sister, lied about playing a game fairly, or didn't tell your parents the truth? *(Still wrapping the kid up.)*

Sometimes you have done something you know you are going to get into trouble for so, in those difficult moments, you might tell what you think is a "little lie." Honestly, there is no such things as a "little lie." A lie is a lie. *(Wrapping kid!)*

Oftentimes, what happens is that once you tell one lie, it's easy to tell

Take It Further

Connect this object lesson to other Bible passages:
- Peter betrays Jesus (Luke 22:54-62)
- Potiphar's Wife (Genesis 39)
- The Ten Commandments (Exodus 20)

another one and another one and another one until you are tangled in a web of lies. *(Child should be very tangled by now.)*

STEP 2: Read Hebrews 12:1.

SAY: This verse tells us to become untangled from sin. Lying is a sin.

STEP 3: Prepare to use scissors to carefully cut the yarn the child is wrapped in.

SAY: Wow, you can see that one lie leads to another and another. We can get so entangled in our sin that it can stop us from being able to do what we should be doing. How can we prevent being tangled up in lies? *(allow answers)* That's right, we should always tell the truth! *(Carefully cut the yarn wrapped around the child.)* You won't be tangled in a web of lies if you always the truth. *(Thank your volunteer and ask them to have a seat.)*

DISCUSSION QUESTIONS

1. Have you ever found yourself wrapped in a tangle of lies?

2. Were there consequences?

3. Would you make a decision to handle that situation the same way again?

LIFE APPLICATION

SAY: Sometimes we find ourselves facing a situation where we think we should lie. We may think something unpleasant will happen if we tell the truth. No matter what, being an honest person is always better then sinning. God will bless us for being honest.

Wrap It Up

SAY: Lying is wrong. Lying only entangles us like being wrapped up in yarn and unable to move. We need to live an honest life, like God wants us to.

Chapter 18: All Puffed Up

Scripture: "Rather, in humility value others above yourselves, not looking to your own interests but each of you to the interest of the others."

– Philippians 2:3b NIV

Topic
Humility

Purpose
To help children discover that a humble spirit isn't prideful.

Type:
Everyday objects

Supplies:
- Sheet of paper with notes
- Uninflated beach ball
- Air pump

Preparation
Prepare note page using items mentioned in Step 1.

Presentation

STEP 1: Enter the presentation area reading the notes you prepared.

1. [Name], you are the best soccer player in the world!
2. [Name], you're the smartest kid I know!
3. [Name], your clothes are to die for!

STEP 2: Stand in front of the group.

SAY: If you're not careful, you can get a little puffed up like this ball. With each compliment you receive, you can begin to think more highly of yourself than you should. We need to remember God made us who we are. He gave us all our talents and abilities. He designed our brain and our looks. Any time you receive a compliment you should be polite, but inside you should give God the thanks for helping you be able. God should get all the glory.

Take It Further

Connect this object lesson to other Bible passages:
- Son of Man came to serve others (Mark 10:45)
- If you are proud you will fall (Proverbs 16:18)
- Put up with one another in love (Ephesians 4:2)

STEP 3: Read Philippians 2:3.

SAY: One simple way to do this is instead of allowing yourself to get puffed up *(pump more air into the ball)*, you can help others see the value they have. We are called to encourage one another. We need to join them in thanking God for his gifts to us. Encourage someone today.

DISCUSSION QUESTIONS

1. Is it easy for you to receive a compliment?
2. Is it easy for you to compliment others?
3. Who is one person that you can encourage this week?

LIFE APPLICATION

SAY: Everyone loves to be told something positive about themselves, but too much of this can help us to lose sight of who really desires the credit. When we give God our thanks and encourage others, we can keep ourselves from becoming too puffed up.

Wrap It Up

SAY: Remember when you receive a compliment to be gracious, but to give God the thanks for the gifts he has given you. Encouraging others and giving God the glory will remind you to be humble and thankful.

Chapter 19: Be One

Scripture: "I looked for someone among them who would build up the wall and stand before me in the gap on behalf of the land so I would not have to destroy it, but I found no one." – Ezekiel 22:30, NIV

Topic
Initiative

Purpose
To help children be brave enough to stand up first or stand alone.

Type:
Action

Supplies:
- 4 wooden or cardboard blocks

Preparation
None.

PRESENTATION

SAY: Marathon runners train to be the best in their sport. They train hard for months and years so that they can be the winner when they compete. They want to win. They want to be first.

STEP 1: Play a game where the children have to be first. Instruct the group to sit in a large circle and place a large wooden or cardboard block in the center. Call out descriptions to see which child can be first to grab the block. (For example, call out kids with brown eyes, kids wearing sneakers, kids wearing red, kids who are in 3rd grade, etc.) Continue until all four blocks have been claimed.

SAY: In that game, you were racing to see who could be first. However, there are other times when people don't want to be first. Let me explain. If you see someone being teased or bullied, it might be hard to be the first one to stand up for them, especially if you might be the only one standing up for them. That would take initiative, which means seeing what needs to be done

Take It Further

Connect this object lesson to other Bible passages:
- Disciples follow Jesus (Matthew 4:18-22)
- God calls Abram (Genesis 12)
- Joshua and the Battle of Jericho (Joshua 5:13-6:27)

Object Lesson: Initiative

and doing it, even if you are the first or only one to act.

STEP 2: Read Ezekiel 22:30.

SAY: God was looking for people to rebuild Israel's walls, to stand for God, but he couldn't find even one person willing to do it. NOT ONE PERSON. That must have made God sad. All that he does for us and no one would step up and do something for him.

There will be times when something wrong is happening and you really think God wants you to do something. What about one of the examples I gave earlier? Let's pretend you see someone being bullied at recess. What could you do? *(Allow answers)* Those are good suggestions. Do you think it would be scary to be the first to step up and be that one person who does the right thing? *(Allow answers)* Sure it could be, but God promises to stand with us and give us courage. When you see something needs to be done, pray for courage and ask God to go with you. He will.

DISCUSSION QUESTIONS

1. Have you ever been the first or only person to do the right thing?

2. How did that feel?

3. What kind of situations might a person your age have to take initiative?

LIFE APPLICATION

SAY: It can be difficult and scary to stand alone when everyone else is making a different choice. Taking initiative means being courageous and brave to do what you believe. Pray to God for help, and never be afraid to stand alone if necessary, or to be the first to stand.

Wrap It Up

SAY: Bad things will happen around you. God calls us to do what is right. Pray for courage and don't be afraid to be the first to stand up and do the right thing.

Chapter 20: Inside Out

Scripture: "Those who do what is right are guided by their honest lives." – Proverbs 11:3a

Topic
Integrity

Purpose
To help the children understand that having integrity means being a trustworthy person.

Type:
Food

Supplies:
- Banana
- Orange
- $5 bill

Preparation
None.

PRESENTATION

STEP 1: Hold up a banana.

SAY: Sometimes it's very easy to look at something and identify what it is. When I see this, I know this is a banana. I bought it from the grocery store next to a sign that said "BANANAS". I've eaten a banana before so I know what a banana looks like. If I peel this banana *(peel the banana)*, I know it'll be a banana on the inside.

STEP 2: Hold up the orange.

SAY: When I see this, I know this is an orange. I bought it from the grocery store next to a sign that said "ORANGES". If I peel this orange, I know it will be an orange and not a banana. The inside matches what I know is on the outside. That's what integrity is.

STEP 3: Read Proverbs 11:3.

SAY: Living an honest life means that what is in your thoughts and in your heart matches what people see you doing on the outside with your words and actions. For instance, one day you are listening to your friend complain about someone that stole

Take It Further

Connect this object lesson to other Bible passages:
- Paul and Silas in jail (Acts 16:16-40)
- Daniel and his friends eat vegetables (Daniel 1)
- Ananias and Sapphira (Acts 5:1-11)

Object Lesson:
Integrity

his pencil. Now you agree that stealing is wrong. You are upset with him. You think that was a terrible thing to do.

Then later that day you are walking and notice that a $5 bill has fallen out of the pocket of the person ahead of you. *(hold up the $5)* You have choices. If you really believe in your heart and mind that stealing is bad, what should you do? *(Allow answers)* That's right, you would call out to the person and give them their money. You would be guided by the right things to do and live that out with your actions.

Another name for this is integrity. When you do the right thing even when no one is looking or may never know. God sees our heart and knows our thoughts and our actions. He knows if we are living out what we really say we believe. God wants to guide us to live an honest life.

DISCUSSION QUESTIONS

1. Is it easy or hard for your actions to match your words?

2. Why do you think that's so?

3. Do you think living an honest life matters? Why or why not?

LIFE APPLICATION

SAY: Living out an honest life makes you a trustworthy person. People want to know that they can trust you and rely on you. Keeping your promises and honoring your words by meaning what you say will help you be a person with integrity.

Wrap It Up

SAY: Take a good look at yourself to see if your actions and thoughts match what you say out loud. God wants to help you be an honest person. Someone with integrity that would do the right thing even if no one was around to see it.

Chapter 21: Joy Balloon

Scripture: *"Our hearts are full of joy because of him. We trust in him, because he is holy."*
— Psalm 33:21

Topic
Joy

Purpose
To help the children discover that the joy God gives can't be taken away.

Type:
Science

Supplies:
- 2 Balloons
- A candle / lighter
- Permanent marker
- Water

Preparation
- Blow up balloon number one, tie off and draw a happy face on it.
- Blow up balloon number two, add about 2 cups of water, tie off and draw a happy face on it.
- Place the candle and lighter on the table in preparation for the lesson.

PRESENTATION

STEP 1: Stand behind your table with the balloons, candle, and lighter. *(Read Psalm 33:21)*

SAY: Today we are talking about keeping our joy. Our verse today tells us to always be joyful, because of having God in our life, but sometimes it is hard to be happy.

STEP 2: Hold up the balloon without the water in it.

SAY: I have a balloon up here that shows someone who is happy. What about this balloon? *(Show the happy face on the other balloon without picking it up.)* That's right also happy.

STEP 3: Pick up the lighter.

SAY: I am going to light this candle. *(Light the candle)* Sometimes things happen that make us sad. Like, if our parents are fighting, or we didn't get a good grade on something we worked hard on. Maybe, a friend is moving or someone you love is sick. Things can happen that can make us sad. So how do we follow this verse? *(Connect to the Bible story if you are*

Take It Further
Connect this object lesson to other Bible passages:
- The joy of the Lord makes you strong (Nehemiah 8:10b)
- My heart jumps for joy (Psalm 28:7)
- Always be joyful (Philippians 4:4)

Object Lesson: Joy

using this lesson with it. For instance, Paul in prison)

So we have this person that is happy *(hold up the balloon with no water)*, at least they look happy on the outside. We are going to pretend this fire is like the bad and challenging things that can come along in life, *(hold balloon over fire – it will pop)* and cause our joy to go away.

STEP 4: Light the candle again. Pick up the second balloon with the water in it.

SAY: Here is another person who is happy. What do you think will happen when I hold this person over the fire? *(Allow answers)* Let's see what happens. *(Hold the balloon over the fire so that the water is over the fire. Don't stay there too long.)* Did this one pop? *(Allow answers)* Why not? *(Allow answers, kids may have noticed the water inside.)* That's right. There is water in this balloon. When I hold the balloon over the fire the water protects it from popping. The balloon is still a happy balloon.

The water in this balloon is like Jesus in us. When we have Jesus in our life he helps us keep our joy. We will still have fire, problems and challenges, *(point to the fire that is still lit)* but when we do what our verse says and choose to rejoice in difficult times, Jesus helps us keep our joy even when things are tough.

DISCUSSION QUESTIONS

1. What can we do to remember to focus on joy when hard things happen?
2. Do you have friends or family who can help remind you to be joyful?
3. What should you do as soon as hard things come?

LIFE APPLICATION

SAY: Hard things are difficult to go through. But when we have Jesus in our life we know that if a hard thing is happening, God is with us when we are going through it.

Wrap It Up

SAY: When we have Jesus in our life he can help us get through difficult things. We need to do our part and try to look for the positive and be joyful even when things are hard.

Chapter 22: Sweet Words

Scripture: "Pleasant words are like honey. They are sweet to the spirit and bring healing to the body."
– Proverbs 16:24

Topic
Kindness

Purpose
To help children see that their words have tremendous power.

Type:
Food

Supplies:
- Jar of honey
- Small bowl
- Spoon

Preparation
None

Bonus idea
Get little honey sticks for the kids, or very tiny sample spoons so they can each taste a small amount of honey.

CAUTION! Make sure there are not allergies. Sometimes children allergic to bee stings will also react to honey. Make sure you inform parents.

PRESENTATION

STEP 1: Hold up a spoon of honey.

SAY: What is this? (*Allow answers*) That's right, it is honey. How many of you like honey? (*show   of hands*) How many of you know that honey is in the Bible? Let's read.

STEP 2: Read Proverbs 16:24.

SAY: How can kind words be like honey? (*Allow answers*) What happens when we say something kind to someone? (*Allow answers*) When we say something kind to someone, it makes them feel special and happy. The Bible says it can actually be healing. Wow, that means words have power.

If a friend is going through a hard time, what might you say to help them feel better? (*Allow answers, it may be necessary to use an example of why they are sad to help them come up with*

Take It Further
Connect this object lesson to other Bible passages:
- The Golden Rule (Luke 6:31)
- The Early Church (Acts 2:42-47)
- Be kind and tender to one another (Ephesians 4:32)

Object Lesson:
Kindness

answers.) What are some things you shouldn't say? *(Allow answers)* Our words are very powerful. They can be used to speak kindness that builds someone up and makes them feel better.

DISCUSSION QUESTIONS

1. What makes a person kind?
2. Do you think others would describe you as kind?
3. What are two ways you can show kindness this week?

LIFE APPLICATION

SAY: Words have power. Kind words go a long way and don't always take a lot of effort. Make a choice to spread a little kindness wherever you go!

Wrap It Up

SAY: God uses us to build each other up and help others feel better. Look for opportunities to say kind things to those around you and be used by God to bring healing to someone's day.

Chapter 23: God First

Scripture: "Love the Lord your God with all your heart and with all your soul and with all your mind and with all your strength." – Mark 12:30, NIV

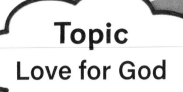

Topic
Love for God

Purpose
To remind children that their love for God should be their top priority over everyone and everything else.

Type:
Everyday objects

Supplies:
- Foam "#1" finger
- Index card
- Permanent marker
- Tape

Preparation
Use the marker to write the words "God First" on the index card. Set the card aside.

PRESENTATION

SAY: Kids your age are bombarded with distractions, right? You have chores, school, sports, practices, and video games to keep you busy! It's very easy to allow these things to be first in our lives.

STEP 1: Put on and hold up the foam finger.

> **SAY:** We enjoy most of the things we do that take up a lot of our time. But there's one person who should not be left out...God.

STEP 2: Read Mark 12:30.

> **SAY:** What is this verse saying? It's saying that we should love God more than anyone or anything else.

STEP 3: Tape the "God First" index card to the tip of the foam finger.

> **SAY:** Putting God first is not always easy to do, but it's what we are commanded to do and what we should

Take It Further

Connect this object lesson to other Bible passages:
- God gave his only Son (John 3:16)
- In all ways obey him (Proverbs 3:6)
- Put God's Kingdom first (Matthew 6:33)

Object Lesson:
Love for God

want to do. If we give other people or other things more time and attention than we give God, life will get out of balance.

Loving God first means just that. You might have to stop doing something or do something less to make God first. It might feel like a huge sacrifice at first. However, when you think about God sacrificing his only son Jesus for you, it'll be totally worth it!

DISCUSSION QUESTIONS

1. Is there someone or something that you love more than God?
2. What can you do to make God more of a priority in your life?

LIFE APPLICATION

SAY: It's very easy to allow distractions to keep us from loving God first and most. God wants you to love him with your whole self. Spend some time in prayer talking to God and ask him to help you love him first and most.

Wrap It Up

SAY: When we think about what we have to do for the day or the week, we should be sure that God is our first priority. He deserves our best.

Chapter 24: Spread the Love

Scripture: "A new command I give you: Love one another. As I have loved you, so you must love another." – John 13:34, NIV

Purpose
To help children see that the love they show to others can also radiate the love of Christ.

Type:
Science

Supplies:
- Paper towel
- Pen
- Water/ dish
- Red marker

Preparation

Using a pen, draw a heart at the bottom of a paper towel. Pour water into dish and have it on the table

Tip

Make sure this is big enough to be seen by everyone. Not so big that the water can't travel to the other hearts in time to finish the lesson.

PRESENTATION

STEP 1: Hold up the paper towel with the heart drawn on it.

SAY: I have a heart drawn here on this paper towel. This heart represents your heart. Without Jesus in your heart it is empty, like this heart. But God gave us a way, through Jesus dying on the cross, to have your heart filled with love. When we accept Jesus as our personal Savior, he fills our heart with love.

STEP 2: Fill in the heart with the red marker.

SAY: What an amazing gift! Jesus gave us a way to be forgiven. We can now have Jesus in our heart and have a relationship with God. But it doesn't end there. In one of the commandments he tells us to love one another.

STEP 3: Draw 2 or 3 more hearts (in pen) right above the red heart. Read John 13:34.

SAY: This verse tells us God gives us this amazing love so we can share it with others.

STEP 4: Touch the bottom of the paper towel to the water. The red marker should begin to climb toward the other hearts.

Take It Further

Connect this object lesson to other Bible passages:
- Love your neighbor (Mark 12:31)
- Love on another (John 15:12)
- Love one another, love comes from God (1 John 4:7)

Object Lesson: Love for Others

SAY: God wants us to share His love. How can we do this? *(Allow answers)* Just like this red from the heart overflowed and poured into the other hearts, when we have Jesus's love in our hearts, it overflows and pours into other people around us.

If your heart is empty today because you haven't accepted Jesus as your personal Savior and received his love, let us know and we can talk to you about it. Today may be the day you fill your heart with Jesus. For those of you that do have Jesus in your heart, be on the look out for ways to show love this week!

TIP: Have small groups of children do this experiment themselves using paper cups.

BONUS IDEA: Brainstorm ways children can show love to others. Create a commitment sheet for them to write in their ideas and remind them to love others.

DISCUSSION QUESTIONS

1. Do you find it easy or difficult to love others?
2. Who is one person you can show love to this week?
3. How does Jesus show us love?

LIFE APPLICATION

SAY: Showing love to those in our community can be done in very practical ways. A heart filled with love for others flows out of God's great love for us. Love God and love others well!

Wrap It Up

SAY: Love one another is a command, not a suggestion or something you do if you feel like it. God calls us to love. He gives us the love we need to share. Find someone to share the love of God with this week.

Chapter 25: Mixed Messages

Scripture: "So God created man in his own likeness. He created him in the likeness of God. He created them as male and female." – Genesis 1:27

Topic
Self-Esteem

Purpose
To compare and contrast the messages the world tells us versus what God tells us.

Type:
Everyday objects

Supplies:
- 2 handheld mirrors
- 2 Sticky notes
- Permanent marker

Preparation
Use the marker to write "WORLD" on one sticky note and "GOD" on the other sticky note. Attach one note to the back of each mirror and then place the mirrors, glass-side up.

Tip
If you don't have enough mirrors for all, use a bigger mirror for each and model this from the stage.

PRESENTATION

SAY: We can sometimes get mixed messages depending on whom we're listening to. If you're at school, your teacher might say, "Stop talking" and then ask you to answer a question. If you're at home, your parent might say, "Leave your brother (or sister) alone" one minute and "I want you to get along" the next. Mixed messages for sure!

STEP 1: Pick up the World mirror.

SAY: The world we live in also sends us mixed messages. *Look into the "WORLD" mirror and talk into it with messages the world gives us, such as:*
- *"You're not enough."*
- *"You'll never be good enough."*
- *"Can't you do anything right?"*
- *"You're a loser."*

Wow. How do you think someone might feel after hearing messages like that? *(Allow answers)*

Take It Further
Connect this object lesson to other Bible passages:
- You created my inner... (Psalm 139:13-14)
- Think of yourself to highly (Romans 12:3)
- God's handiwork (Ephesians 2:10)

STEP 2: Pick up the "God" mirror.

SAY: What if we listened to God's messages instead? Look into the "GOD" mirror and talk into it with messages he gives us, such as:

- *"You are precious to me."*
- *"You are loved."*
- *"You are a gift to the world."*
- *"You are made in my image."*

STEP 3: Put the mirrors down.

SAY: What a difference! God doesn't give us mixed messages. His words and thoughts toward us never change, no matter what we do. He wants us to know that we are made in his image. That we are precious to him. That he has placed us here to be used for good. We were made to reflect God and not believe the lies of the world.

DISCUSSION QUESTIONS

1. How does it feel to know that you're made in God's image?
2. What might cause you to not believe that?
3. How can you tune out the lies the world tells you?

LIFE APPLICATION

SAY: The world tells us one thing and God tells us the opposite. It can be hard to know what voice to listen to. We learn how God loves us when we pray, read the Bible and hang out with other Christians.

Wrap It Up

SAY: We hear about not being enough in all the messages around us. God wants us to spend more time listening to what he says about us. Remember who you are in his image. Live your life out knowing you are loved and precious to him.

Chapter 26: **Twisted Up in Lies**

Scripture: "Dear children, let us not love with words or speech but with actions and in truth."
– 1 John 3:18, NIV

Topic
Lying/ Dishonesty

Purpose
To help children understand that God wants them to be honest.

Type:
Everyday objects

Supplies:
- Flashlight
- 1 play tunnel

Preparation
Set up the play tunnel where you will teach.

PRESENTATION

STEP 1: With flashlight in hand, stand next to a play tunnel.

SAY: I love to explore! I mean, I love to go on really cool adventures! *(Turn on the flashlight)* I love to look in dark places and *(crawl through play tunnel with the flashlight on but do not exit)* I love to crawl through tight spaces to look for really small things. Crawling through tight spaces means I have to twist and turn to fit those small spaces. Sometimes, I even get stuck.

STEP 2: Pop your head out of the structure but leave your body in. Act stuck. Have fun with it.

SAY: That makes me think of other twists and turns that we can take to reach a certain destination. One of the shortcuts we can take is lying. Yeah, we know lying is wrong, but sometimes, telling a wee little lie doesn't matter, right? *(Allow answers)* It can be easy to do, especially when we don't think we'll

Take It Further

Connect this object lesson to other Bible passages:
- The Ten Commandments (Exodus 20)
- Be Trustworthy (Proverbs 12:22)
- Pure talk (Ephesians 4:29)

get caught. But what happens when we get caught? One lie turns into another lie, which turns into another lie.

STEP 3: Struggle in the play tunnel.

SAY: We can get so twisted up in lies that we might not even know the real truth anymore! You may feel stuck. What can you do? *(Allow answers)* What we need to do if we have told a lie is pray. *(Come out of the tunnel)* We need to ask God to forgive us. This is called confessing. You need to ask the person you lied to for forgiveness. Then you make the decision to be an honest person.

When you feel tempted to lie, pray for God to help you be an honest person so you don't get all twisted and stuck. Make the decision today to be honest.

DISCUSSION QUESTIONS

1. Have you ever told a lie? How did that feel?

2. Have you ever been told a lie? How did it feel?

3. What steps did you have to take after you lied or were told a lie?

LIFE APPLICATION

SAY: The easy way out of a hard situation might be to tell a lie, but it never turns out well. You always lose when you lie.

Wrap It Up

SAY: It's easy for us to get ourselves into tricky situations, and we think that telling a lie is the easy way out. You will likely have to ask forgiveness (from God and from the person you lied to) and you might have to earn back someone's trust. It might be hard, but it can be done.

Chapter 27: World-Wide Message

Scripture: "But you will receive power when the Holy Spirit comes on you; and you will be my witnesses in Jerusalem, and in all Judea and Samaria, and to the ends of the earth." – Acts 1:8, NIV

Topic
Missions

Purpose
To help children understand that God's love is meant to be shared all around the world.

Type:
Kid-Volunteer

Supplies:
- Inflatable globe
- Heart stickers
- Pictures of any missionaries your church supports

Preparation
- Blow up globe
- Prepare pictures of missionaries and have up front (perhaps place these photos on a board/easel for easy viewing.)

Bonus idea
Make prayer cards about your missionaries for the children to take home.

PRESENTATION

STEP 1: Hold up the globe and talk with the children about places they've visited.

SAY: Who can tell me some places they have traveled to. *(Point to the places they've been on the globe.)* Traveling to different places can be new and exciting! There are fun things to see and do, great food to be enjoyed, and new memories to be made. Most of the time when people travel, they do so for vacation, to rest and relax. Some people travel for work. Some people travel to share the news of Jesus with people who might not know about him. Those people are called missionaries. They go out on missions from God to share his love.

STEP 2: Point to pictures of the missionaries.

SAY: Our church has (insert number of missionaries) missionaries sent out all around the world. Here are some of our

Take It Further

Connect this object lesson to other Bible passages:
- The Great Commission (Matthew 28:19-20)
- Tell About Jesus (1 Chronicles 16:24)
- Go into all the world (Mark 16:15)

missionaries. They have traveled to *(insert the countries they are in).* Let's see where that is on the globe.

STEP 3: Call out a missionary and point to where they are on the globe.

SAY: Our missionaries are in these countries sharing the love of God with the people there. Let's place a heart sticker on each spot our missionaries are at.

STEP 4: Invite children up to place heart stickers on the places where your missionaries serve.

SAY: Being a missionary is hard work. They are away from everyone and everything they know. They do it because they love God and know he wants them there. They are courageous. We can help them with our prayers and support. You can be a missionary when you grow up and help people know God. You can be a missionary right now by sharing about Jesus with your friends and family.

DISCUSSION QUESTIONS

1. How can we support missionaries around the world?
2. Do you think missionaries have to go around the world to share God's love with others?
3. In what ways can you be a missionary right here where you live?

LIFE APPLICATION

SAY: When we have good news to share, we want to shout it out so that everyone hears! Knowing that Jesus loves us, died for our sins, and wants us to live with him forever is the best news for us to share with everyone, near and far.

Wrap It Up

SAY: Being a missionary sometimes means going to faraway places, but you can be a missionary right where you live, go to school, and even go to church. We can support missionaries around the world with our love, prayer, and support (giving money, time, and supplies). We can be a missionary in our community by being sharing what Jesus has done for us, helping our neighbors, loving our friends, and serving others.

Chapter 28: A Recipe in Obedience

Scripture: "He replied, 'Instead, blessed are those who hear God's word and obey it.'" – Luke 11:28

Topic
Obedience

Purpose
To help children understand that obedience is a choice to do the right thing.

Type:
Food

Supplies:

- Canister of powdered lemonade drink mix
- Plastic pitcher
- Water (cold or with ice)
- Large spoon
- Cups

Preparation

Place all the items you need to make the lemonade on your table up front.

PRESENTATION

STEP 1: Show children all the items you have to make your lemonade.

SAY: Ok, here we go. I have everything I need here to make lemonade *(show items as you call them out)*: my lemonade mix, a pitcher, some cold water and a spoon. Let's see *(look confused)*...what should I do first? Maybe I should pour the water into the mix and shake it up...*(allow the children to respond)*. Maybe I should just pour some of the mix in my mouth and then drink some water...*(allow the children to respond)*.

Hmmm...decisions, decisions. So many decisions! Every day, we have a choice. We can do things the easy way or the hard way. We can do things the right way or the wrong way. We can do things our way and not God's way. So many decisions.

One choice we have to make every day is the choice to obey. When you're a

Take It Further

Connect this object lesson to other Bible passages:

- Noah's Ark (Genesis 6)
- Obey Your Parents (Ephesians 6:1-3)
- The Ten Commandments (Exodus 20)

Object Lesson:
Obedience

grown up, you can make the choice to obey the stop sign or not. When you're a kid, you can make the choice to follow your parent's instructions or not. In those examples, if you don't make the right choice, there could be serious consequences.

Today, I wanted to make lemonade. I thought about making it my own way. What do you think would happen if I followed the instructions on the container? Do you think my lemonade would taste the way it's supposed to? *(Allow answers.)*

STEP 2: Read Luke 11:28.

SAY: When we read God's Word, the Bible, and follow what it says we will be blessed. God lays out ways for our life to go according to his plan. He directs us to do the right things.

STEP 3: Make a pitcher of lemonade according to the package instructions. Share the lemonade with all the children.

SAY: Yum, I am glad I followed the instructions. This is how lemonade is supposed to turn out. Our life turns out the way it is supposed to, when we obey God.

DISCUSSION QUESTIONS

1. Have you ever struggled with doing things your own way?
2. Who do you need to obey more?
3. How can you be more obedient?

LIFE APPLICATION

SAY: Obedience is a choice. Those who tell us what to do want the very best for us and want to keep us safe and healthy.

Wrap It Up

SAY: When you choose not to obey because you think your way is better is being disobedient. Obedience involves trusting the person giving the directions and honoring them by doing what they say.

Chapter 29: Popping Patience

Scripture: "Wait for the Lord Be strong and don't lose hope. Wait for the Lord." – Psalm 27:14

Topic
Patience

Purpose
To illustrate that patience really does pay off.

Type:
Food

Supplies:

- Box of microwave popcorn
- Napkins or cups to give popcorn to children

OPTION:
Place a Microwave in the room – Pop popcorn during the lesson

Preparation

Pre-pop a bag of popcorn and open it before class. Pass through the room and spread the aroma around. Pop enough popcorn for all the children to have some. (set it out of sight)

PRESENTATION

SAY: How many of you can smell something in the room? What do you smell? *(Allow answers)* That's right, popcorn. When you walk in here and smell popcorn what do you think is going to happen? *(Allow answers)* You think you are going to get to eat some popcorn. You are right, but you have to wait. How many of you know what popcorn tastes like? *(Show of hands)* When you smell that popcorn, can you recall what it tastes like? Does it make you want it now? Waiting is hard. Sometimes, God needs us to wait before he gives us an answer to a prayer or helps us solve a problem. When we are in a tough place and we ask God for help, sometimes it feels like he isn't doing anything.

STEP 1: Start popping the popcorn in the microwave now, if you are using that option.

> **SAY:** God is always working in the background. Sometimes we don't see what he is doing. We only know that isn't happening fast like we want.
>
> God wants us to trust him. To believe that even when we don't see what he is doing he is helping us. When we trust him we can wait with a happy feeling, like you have when you smell the

Take It Further

Connect this object lesson to other Bible passages:
- Abraham and Sarah (Genesis 18:1-15)
- The Prodigal Son (Luke 15:11-24)
- The Fruit of the Spirit (Galatians 5:22-23)

 Top 50 Object Lessons: Games & Activities

Object Lesson: Patience

popcorn and know you are going to get some. You have to wait, but you know something good is going to come at the end. You don't have to wait and worry. You can wait and be excited and hopeful about what he is bringing.

So the next time you pray and ask God to help you with something, believe/expect you are getting helped, even if you have to wait. Just like that lovely smell tells you that popcorn is coming, when you pray, remember to expect that God is bringing something good.

STEP 2: Hand out popcorn to all the children.

DISCUSSION QUESTIONS

1. When are times you have to wait for things?
2. Is it easy or hard for you to wait?
3. What can you do to be a more patient person?

LIFE APPLICATION

SAY: The next time you pray and ask God to help you, remember the smell of popcorn and when you knew the popcorn was coming. It may still be hard to wait, but you knew you would get the popcorn in the end. Just like you can know God will hear your prayer and give you something good in the end.

Wrap It Up

SAY: Waiting is hard. We want what we want when we want it, but God doesn't want us to see it that way. He wants us to grow in our patience because he has things he wants to teach us and things he wants us to see that we might miss because we're so impatient.

Chapter 30: Peace Covering

Scripture: "Christ himself is our peace..."
– Ephesians 2:14

Topic
Peace

Purpose
To illustrate that God's peace covers us all.

Type:
Kid-involved
Game

Supplies:
- Large kids' parachute
- Foam or soft playground balls

Preparation

Lay out the parachute so that it's flat on the floor. Have the children sit around the parachute. (If you have a large group, use more than one parachute to ensure everyone has a spot of the parachute to grab.)

PRESENTATION

SAY: How many of you have ever been on a sailboat? *(Allow answers.)* What happens when a strong wind blows while you're on the boat? *(Allow answers.)*

STEP 1: Have the children stand up and grab a piece of the parachute. Instruct them to not shake it at this point.

SAY: Sometimes, we can find that life is the same way. We go along our merry way and life is calm. Everything is great. Then all of a sudden things come at us that almost make us fall down!

STEP 2: Instruct the children to begin raising and lowering the parachute to make it rocky.

SAY: School work becomes challenging, we don't make a school team, someone we love becomes sick, a friend moves away, things get thrown at us really fast.

Take It Further

Connect this object lesson to other Bible passages:
- Jesus calms the storm (Mark 4:35-41)
- Perfect peace (Isaiah 26:3)
- Be a peacemaker (Matthew 5:9)

STEP 3: Toss a few of the balls onto the parachute while the children continue to raise and lower it. Instruct the children to stop shaking the parachute and be seated.

> **SAY:** These things can really affect us. It may feel crazy and out of control. We might even wonder why God allows bad things to happen in the first place.
>
> So what can we do when we feel that life is too chaotic? We can pray. When we pray we talk to God about how we feel. When we talk to God we remember he is with us.

STEP 4: Have the children lift the parachute over them and sit on the inside edge. The entire parachute should cover the group as if they were sitting in a tent. *(Read Ephesians 2:14)*

> **SAY:** The Bible tells us that Christ is our peace. He himself will cover us with his peace. His covering is a safe place from whatever we may face. When we feel things are crazy or scary, remember to talk to Jesus. He will cover you with protection and peace.

DISCUSSION QUESTIONS

1. Is your life peaceful or not peaceful right now?

2. How have you handled not peaceful times?

3. What about today's lesson can you take away and remember?

LIFE APPLICATION

SAY: No matter what we face, Christ is our peace. He can calm our hearts and help us to get through really tough times. Our job is to trust him and receive his peace.

Wrap It Up

SAY: Life may be hard for you right now. You might feel hopeless and helpless. Can you trust God? Pray to God and let him fill you with peace. (End by reading Matthew 15:13 "May the God who gives hope fill you with great joy. May you have perfect peace as you trust in him. May the power of the Holy Spirit fill you with hope.")

Chapter 31: Matter of Attraction

Scripture: "Don't let anyone fool you. 'Bad companions make a good person bad.'"

– 1 Corinthians 15:33

Topic
Peer Pressure

Type:
Science

Purpose
To help children understand that peer pressure is not always bad.

Supplies:
- A variety of small magnets
- One larger magnet

Preparation

Lay the small magnets on the table.

PRESENTATION

SAY: I'm so glad that when we come to church, we're among friends. It's always a lot of fun to be around friends, isn't it? *(Allow answers)* It is such a blessing to have friends to hang out with and learn with.

Today we are going to talk about friends. It is important to realize that we are influenced by the people around us. Who knows what the word "influenced" means? *(Allow answers)* Influence means when someone changes or sways our choices. When we hang around with people, we tend to do what they do and say what they say. If we choose good friends, that are making the right choices, then following them would be wise.

STEP 1: Hold up the bigger magnet.

SAY: I have some magnets up here. Let's pretend that these magnets are all of us. As this magnet moves around, it collects other magnets (friends).

Take It Further

Connect this object lesson to other Bible passages:
- Don't Follow the Crowd (Proverbs 1:10)
- Don't Follow the Crowd (Exodus 23:2)
- Walk with the Wise (Proverbs 13:20)

Object Lesson: Peer Pressure

STEP 2: Take the large magnet and start collecting a trail of small magnets, by passing the large magnet past all the small ones.

SAY: This is how it is with our friends. We tend to move along together. That is why it is so important that we pick our friends well.

STEP 3: Read 1 Corinthians 15:33.

SAY: This verse tells us that if we pick bad friends we will be encouraged by them to do the wrong things.

STEP 4: Hold up the small magnet.

SAY: Sometimes we are the small magnets and we are part of a group of friends.

STEP 5: Hold up the large magnet.

SAY: Sometimes people are following us. Either way, we have choices to make. We need to choose to do the right things and we need to choose the right friends, because we are not alone in life. We influence each other. You need to respect the power that those around us have on us, and that we have on others.

DISCUSSION QUESTIONS

?

1. What kind of friends do you attract?
2. Do your friends help you to make good decisions?
3. If not, what might need to change in order for that to happen?

LIFE APPLICATION

SAY: Having a friend means being a friend. Having a good friend means being a good friend. We can help our friends make good choices and we should seek out friends to help us do the same.

Wrap It Up

SAY: Whom you choose to surround yourself with can determine the kind of decisions you make. You can have friends who encourage you to make poor choices or you can seek out friends who will encourage you to make positive choices. It's up to you.

Chapter 32: Up, Up, Up

Scripture: "Don't worry about anything. Instead, tell God about everything. Ask and pray. Give thanks to him. – Philippians 4:6

Topic
Prayer

Purpose

To demonstrate what happens when we release our prayers to God.

Type:

Science

Supplies:

- Bubbles

Preparation

None.

PRESENTATION

SAY: Tell me a little bit about what you know about prayer. *(Allow answers).* Prayer is when we go to God and praise him for who he is and what he's done, ask for forgiveness for what we've done wrong, thank him for our blessings and ask him for help.

STEP 1: Pick up bubbles.

SAY: I have some bubbles here. I am going to blow some bubbles and I want you to watch what they do. *(Blow bubbles)* Do all the bubbles eventually pop? *(Allow answers)* Do they all pop at the same time? *(Allow answers)* All of these bubbles popped, but some lasted longer than others. We are going to pretend that these are our prayers.

STEP 2: Blow more bubbles. (Tip: Don't blow them out over the kids so you can maintain control)

SAY: We blow our prayers into the bubbles and they head out to God. When they pop, we are going to pretend that this is when God answers the prayers. Just like these bubbles go up, so do our prayers. Some bubbles stay intact longer while some

Take It Further

Connect this object lesson to other Bible passages:

- The Lord's Prayer (Matthew 6:9-13)
- Go to God in Prayer (1 John 5:14-15)
- Keep on Praying (Ephesians 6:18)

popped quickly. This can remind us that while God hears all of our prayers, some prayers take a longer time to be answered than others.

Does God give us everything we pray for? No, just like our parents have to sometimes say NO because that is what is best for us to be healthy and safe. God has to say NO sometimes too.

So even if you think your prayer isn't being answered because you didn't get what you wanted, it may have been answered and God said NO. God only answers three ways. YES, NO, or WAIT. But God always answers our prayers. Just like these bubbles always pop. God's answer is always what is the very best for us, because he loves us.

DISCUSSION QUESTIONS

1. Are you worried about something?
2. Have you prayed about it?
3. Has praying about something ever made you worry less?

LIFE APPLICATION

SAY: Praying helps us to remember that God is in control. No matter what we face, we can go to God in prayer.

Wrap It Up

Releasing our prayers to God releases our control over situations and helps us to depend on God in ways beyond our own strength. We have to remember that sometimes the answer isn't YES , but WAIT or NO. Trust God and he will take care of you.

Chapter 33: Balance Act

Scripture: "Trust in the Lord with all your heart. Do not depend on your own understanding. In all your ways remember him. Then he will make your paths smooth and straight." – Proverbs 3:5-6

Topic Priorities

Purpose
To demonstrate that determining priorities requires balancing.

Type:
Everyday objects

Supplies:
- Balancing scale
- Marbles
- Sticky notes

Preparation
Place a sticky note that says "God Time" on one RIGHT side of the scale so the children can see it. Place a sticky note that says "Other Time" on the LEFT side of the scale so the children can see it.

Alternate Idea:
If you don't have a scale, tie same size plastic storage bowls to strings hanging from two sides of a stick or dowel.

PRESENTATION

SAY: Life can keep us pretty busy, right? We're going this place and that place at the speed of light. If we're not careful, we can take on too much and it might make our lives be out of balance. Let me demonstrate this for you.

STEP 1: Stand behind the balancing scale while holding the marbles.

> **SAY:** I have two sides to this scale. One side is what the Bible tells us to spend time doing to have a strong relationship with God. The other side is all the other things that happen in life. Let's start with what we have to do. Go to school or schoolwork. *(Put one marble on the left side)*, take care of your pet *(put one marble on the left side)*. You have to eat, sleep, and bathe *(put only one marble on the left side for all three)*, You do chores around your house *(add a marble to the left side)*.

STEP 2: Move over to the other side of the scale.

> **SAY:** What about this side? What about time to pray, *(add a marble to the right side)*, reading your Bible,

Take It Further

Connect this object lesson to other Bible passages:
- The Lord's Prayer (Matthew 6:9-13)
- Go to God in Prayer (1 John 5:14-15)
- Keep on Praying (Ephesians 6:18)

 Top 50 Object Lessons: Games & Activities

(add a marble to the right side), going to church *(add a marble to the right side),* and serving God in some way like picking up trash in your neighborhood *(add a marble to the right side),* or helping at church. *(add a marble to the right side).* Maybe you spend time memorizing a scripture each week. *(add a marble to the right side).*

STEP 2: Look closely at the scale.

SAY: I have done what I have too and what God's wants me to do. It looks like I can add some extra to my 'Other Side.' Maybe an extra-curricular activity like sports or dance, *(Add a marble to the left side),* or hanging out with my friends. *(Add a marble to the left side.)*

So what do we have here? Do things look evenly balanced to you? What if we decide to spend hours online or playing video games? *(Add marbles to the left side)* What happens? *(Allow answers).* What might we have to do to get things balanced out? *(Allow answers).* Sometimes we have to choose to do less things that aren't God things to make more time for God.

DISCUSSION QUESTIONS

1. Do you feel like you balance your activities well?
2. Are you doing too many activities and not enough with God?
3. What might you need to do more or less of?

LIFE APPLICATION

SAY: Life offers so many cool things to do and be part of, but if we take on too much (even if they're good things), life can get out of balance.

Wrap It Up

SAY: Keeping life in balance can be difficult to juggle. There are times that will be busier than others. The key is to do your best, with God's help, to keep doing what's important and readjust things that aren't as important.

Chapter 34: Plugged In

Scripture: "...you will know [God's] great power. It can't be compared with anything else. It is at work for us who believe." – Ephesians 1:19a-b

Topic
Relationship with God

Purpose
To help children see that a relationship with God should be a growing relationship.

Type:
Science

Supplies:
- Window box fan (be sure to be near an electrical outlet, as you will plug in the fan (Substitute a heater if it is cold.)

Preparation

None.

PRESENTATION

SAY: Man it is hot today. Fortunately, I have a fan here to help us cool off. Let me turn it on.

STEP 1: Making sure the fan is unplugged, mess with the controls and look confused.

> **SAY:** Hmm, there seems to be something wrong. It isn't working. Why isn't it working? *(Kids will be answering by now)* Oh, it isn't plugged in. Many things we use every day only work if they're plugged into a power source. What are some things that need to be plugged in for them to work? *(Allow answers.)*

> This fan can provide cool air, but only if it's plugged into a power source. Otherwise, it won't work the way that it's intended to. The same is true of us and our relationship to God.

STEP 2: Read Ephesians 1:19a-b

> **SAY:** His power works for us and in us. God is the source of power in our lives.

Take It Further

Connect this object lesson to other Bible passages:
- The Vine and the Branches (John 15:1-8)
- Have Faith (Hebrews 11:6)
- Bloom where you're planted (Psalm 1:1-3)

Object Lesson:
Relationship with God

If we don't plug into him each day, we won't operate the way we're designed to. So how can we plug into God? Here are a few suggestions:

- We can pray. Seeking God in prayer reminds us that God is in control of our lives, and not us.
- We can read our Bible. God's Word is the ultimate source of what living a Christian life should look like. How can we know how to live if we don't open up his Word?
- We can attend church. Being with other people who desire to live like Jesus can encourage us to do the same.
- We can give. God wants us to give out of the abundance that he's given us, so we can give time and money to help God's work be accomplished here and around the world.

STEP 3: Plug in the fan and turn it on.

SAY: There we go. It is so nice when something does what it was designed to do. Plug into God everyday and see what God can do with you and your life.

DISCUSSION QUESTIONS

1. Do you feel that you're growing in your relationship with Jesus?
2. How are you doing that?
3. What is one thing you can do this week to help you know Jesus better?

LIFE APPLICATION

SAY: When we plug into the greatest power source that exists (God), he will send his presence to live in us and through us so that we can grow in our relationship with him.

Wrap It Up

SAY: If we want to grow in our relationship with God, we have to be connected to him and stay connected to him. He can help us grow into the person he created us to be.

Chapter 35: Make a U-Turn

Scripture: "From that time on Jesus began to preach. 'Turn away from your sins!' he said. 'The kingdom of heaven is near.'" – Matthew 4:17

Topic
Repentance

Purpose

To help children understand that repentance means turning away from sin and turning toward God.

Type:

Everyday objects

Supplies:

- A variety of road signs (be sure to have a U-Turn and a "No U-Turn" sign)

Preparation

Print out your road signs in advance of your presentation.

PRESENTATION

SAY: If you spend as much time in the car as I do, then you are probably very familiar with road signs.

STEP 1: Hold up the road signs, one at time, saving the "No U-Turn" sign for last.

SAY: What do each of these signs means? *(Allow answers)* These signs help drivers stay safe and alert on the road. If there were no signs, there would be chaos. In our Christian faith, we have to stay alert about things coming our way. Let's talk a little more about this sign.

STEP 2: Hold up the "No U-Turn" sign.

SAY: This sign means that you cannot turn around to go back the other way. If we think about that from God's perspective, he wants us to turn around and go back when we make poor choices. That turning back is called repentance. Repentance means turning from sin and turning toward God.

Take It Further

Connect this object lesson to other Bible passages:

- Jesus eats with sinners (Luke 5:27-32)
- Jesus appears to his disciples (Luke 24:36-49)
- John the Baptist Prepares the Way (Matthew 3:1-12)

Object Lesson:
Repentance

STEP 3: Read Matthew 4:17.

SAY: Jesus tells us to turn away from our sin. We have to make the decision to stop.

STEP 4: Hold up the U-Turn sign.

SAY: Each of us makes decisions every day that are either right or wrong. If we make wrong choices, we need to tell God that we're sorry and ask him to help us. This is what the word repent means. We make a U-Turn and head the right way making better choices the next time.

DISCUSSION QUESTIONS

1. Are you aware when you make wrong choices?
2. What do you feel when you make a wrong choice?
3. Is there something in your life that you need God to help you not do anymore?

LIFE APPLICATION

SAY: We all make mistakes, but it's up to us to ask for forgiveness and God's help to not repeat those mistakes. If we ask his forgiveness, he will forgive us (1 John 1:9).

Wrap It Up

SAY: Repenting, or making a U-Turn from sin and turning toward God, helps us to live the life God wants us to live. Once we make the choice to turn away, we are forgiven and free to live life to the fullest!

Chapter 36: Ready for Battle

Scripture: "Put on all of God's armor. Then you can stand ifrm against the devil's evil plans."

– Ephesians 6:11

Purpose

To illustrate the importance of scripture memory.

Type:

Kid-volunteer

Supplies:

- Bible
- Blank pieces of paper
- Marker

Preparation

Use the marker to write the following on the pieces of paper:

- Doubt
- Fear
- Temptation
- Loneliness

PRESENTATION

STEP 1: Begin the presentation by calling out easy addition and multiplication facts.

SAY: I bet some of you have memorized some of those facts for math class, right? Why do you have to memorize math facts? *(Allow answers).* That's right. One day, knowing those facts will help you to make sure that you aren't cheated when you get change back from the store. Knowing them will also help you to be prepared in the future. They're like building blocks. The same is true when we think about memorizing scripture verses. Knowing scripture verses helps us to be ready for whatever comes our way.

STEP 2: Read Ephesians 6:11.

SAY: How do we armor up like it says here? One of the ways is to memorize scripture.

STEP 3: Invite 4 children to come up to the front of the room. Hold up the pieces of paper that you've prepared.

Take It Further

Connect this object lesson to other Bible passages:

- Lamp & Light (Psalm 119:105)
- All Scripture is God-Breathed (2 Timothy 3:16)
- Hide God's Word in Your Heart (Psalm 119:11)

SAY: These papers show just a few of the things that kids your age might have to battle against. These are pretty serious things. Knowing scripture doesn't mean that we won't have to deal with these issues, but being able to recall Bible verses can help us to deal with these things better. They can help us get ready for the battles we'll face.

STEP 4: Give each volunteer a piece of paper and instruct them to ball up their paper. Grab your Bible. When you give the signal, have the volunteers throw their paper ball at you while you use the Bible to protect yourself. You could also quote scripture about those topics while you're 'in the battle.'

SAY: My sword and shield (my Bible) helped me to fight off doubt, fear, temptation, and loneliness. I couldn't keep from being attacked, but my Bible helped me to be ready to fight. That's why memorizing scripture is so important. We'll be able to recall verses when we deal with a variety of issues.

DISCUSSION QUESTIONS

1. Is it easy for you to memorize things?

2. How many Bible verses would you say you know by heart?

3. Why do you think memorizing Bible verses might be important?

LIFE APPLICATION

SAY: Recalling Bible verses from memory can help us when we face difficult situations. We'll be ready for whatever comes our way.

Wrap It Up

SAY: You may not think memorizing Bible verses can make a difference in your life, but if you hide God's Word in your heart, you can be sure that they'll help you deal with difficult situations. It'll be worth it!

Chapter 37: Me, Myself, and I

Scripture: "Turn my heart toward your statutes and not toward selfish gain." – Psalm 119:36, NIV

Topic
Selfishness

Purpose
To illustrate how focusing too much on yourself can cause you to not see the good in other people.

Type:
Everyday objects

Supplies:
- Helium balloon
- Weights (Sold where the balloons are)
- Poster board

Preparation
Get the balloon filled and have it for class.

Tip
If you have a morning class, try and get the balloon as late in the day the day before so it is still floating well.

PRESENTATION

STEP 1: Hold up the balloon.

SAY: I have a balloon here. I want you to think with me for a minute about this balloon. If I let go of this balloon it will float effortlessly around. Imagine if you will, that when we are right with God and we have Jesus and the Holy Spirit filling us inside, we are just like this balloon. We are free to move wherever God needs us, and be able to enjoy the freedom of being close to God.

STEP 2: Pick up a weight.

Have you ever been with someone that always wanted to go first, someone that thought they were the best at everything, someone that never let you pick what game to play? Well when we act like that it is called being selfish. Wanting to put what we want before other people.

SELFISH

STEP 3: Put a weight on the balloon.

Take It Further
Connect this object lesson to other Bible passages:
- Don't Think Highly of Yourself (Romans 12:3)
- The Prodigal Son (Luke 15:11-32)
- Judas Betrays Jesus (Luke 22)

Object Lesson: Selfishness

SAY: Each time we demand to have our own way it is like placing a weight on this balloon. Maybe you brag about how great you are at something making someone else feel bad, *(Add a weight)* or you won't let your friend pick what game to play. *(Add a weight)* Suddenly, you feel less of that spirit of Jesus and freedom and more weighted down. I have filled myself up with me. *(Show how the balloon no longer can float around.)* I can barely move this balloon. I can't go where God wants me, I am too busy being right here filled with me.

STEP 4: Read Psalm 119:36.

SAY: If you find out you are focusing more on what you want, what can you do? *(Allow answers)* That's right, you can pray and ask God to forgive you and start putting others first. Then you become selfless, not selfish. *(Cut o˜ the weights)*

DISCUSSION QUESTIONS

1. Have you ever been a selfish person?
2. What can we do to be less selfish?
3. How can we show others God is more important than getting our way?

LIFE APPLICATION

SAY: Sometimes, we can let our own selves get in the way of being happy and close to God. If we take the focus off of ourselves and care about others, we will be so much happier and make God happy too.

Wrap It Up

SAY: It's great to be confident in yourself. After all, you can do whatever you put your mind too. But if you allow yourself to become too focused on yourself, you will miss out on seeing the great things God can accomplish in your life.

Chapter 38: May I Help You?

Scripture: "Be like the Son of Man. He did not come to be served. Instead, he came to serve others."
– Matthew 20:28

Topic
Service

Purpose
To help children understand how they can serve others.

Type:
Everyday objects
Food

Supplies:
- Garden rake
- Trash bag
- Chocolate chip cookies on a plate (be sure somewhere you have enough for all the kids to have some.)
- Any child toy

Preparation

Place the items in sight at the front where you will teach.

PRESENTATION

STEP 1: Read Matthew 20:28.

SAY: Jesus wants us to serve others. He modeled it for us while he was on the earth.

STEP 2: Hold up a rake and trash bag.

SAY: I have some things in my hand that can be a tool for sharing God's love. What are they? *(Allow answers)* We all have neighbors. Imagine if you will, you find out one of your neighbors has been in the hospital. He'll be ok, but once he comes home, he'll have to stay off of his feet for six whole weeks. That's a bummer. How could you use these to show him God's love? *(Allow answers)* That's right, you could help him keep up with his yard until he gets better.

STEP 3: Hold up the chocolate chip cookies.

Take It Further

Connect this object lesson to other Bible passages:
- One Body, Many Parts (Romans 12:4-6)
- Gifts of the Spirit (1 Corinthians 12)
- Jesus as a Servant (Philippians 2:6-7)

Object Lesson:
Service

SAY: I know you know what these are. How could these be used as a tool to show others that God loves them? *(Allow answers)* You could welcome a new neighbor and invite them to church. You could bring them to an older person who doesn't have many people visiting them. You could take them to a nursing home and share them while visiting people who don't get visitors. You can give them to teachers or important people in your life to tell them how much you appreciate them.

STEP 4: Pass out the cookies while you explore more serving options.

SAY: What are some other ways you can serve people as kids and show the love of God? *(Allow answers)* You could clean at the church, take out someone's trash, or help a friend do a difficult task. There are many things a kid can do to serve God.

DISCUSSION QUESTIONS

1. What does it mean to serve?

2. What do you do that serves others?

3. What should be our attitude as we serve others?

LIFE APPLICATION

SAY: Serving others means taking time to give a little bit of yourself to help someone in need. Serving others is one way to share the love of Jesus while doing something practical to bless someone.

Wrap It Up

SAY: You are never too young to help serve someone else. God wants us to live in community with others and sometimes, that means serving them instead of looking out for ourselves.

Chapter 39: Shout It Out

Scripture: "For I am not ashamed of the gospel, because it is the power of God that brings salvation to everyone who believes." – Romans 1:16a, NIV

Topic
Sharing Faith

Purpose

To encourage children to be bold and share the greatest news of all time.

Type:
Everyday objects

Supplies:
- White t-shirt
- Fabric marker

Preparation

Before the presentation, use the fabric marker to write or draw Christian words or images all over the front and back of the T-shirt. (Cross, Bible, church, praying hands, Christian, love, peace, forgiveness, salvation, etc.)

PRESENTATION

STEP 1: Wear the T-shirt when teaching the lesson.

SAY: Hey everybody! I see everyone is looking quite nice today! I see some pretty awesome sneakers, some nice pants, and even a few fancy hair bows. I also see some cool T-shirts in the room. Read some of the T-shirts in the room if someone has some with print on them. Do you like my T-shirt? Let me tell you a little bit about it. It's certainly one-of-a-kind.

STEP 2: Go over each word and symbol.

SAY: What is on my shirt? *(Review what you wrote.)* Everywhere you turn there are messages. I see so many messages printed on T-shirts and hats, messages that are positive and some not so positive. I feel like the message in my heart is the greatest message of all - Jesus loves you and wants you to be with him for eternity. I could shout it out a million times!

Take It Further

Connect this object lesson to other Bible passages:
- The Great Commission (Matthew 28:16-20)
- I am Not Ashamed (Romans 1:16)
- Jesus is the Way (John 14:6)

(Loudly shout, "Jesus loves you and wants you to be with him for eternity!")

What are some other ways we can tell people about the love of Jesus? *(Allow answers)* There are many ways we can do this. We can bring our friends to church, share what we learned in church with our friends, and invite friends to special events.

STEP 3: Read Romans 1:16a.

SAY: We should always be ready to tell others about what Jesus is to us and what he has done.

DISCUSSION QUESTIONS

1. Do you talk about being a Christian with family, friends, and strangers?
   - If yes, what makes you do that? Do you feel comfortable?
   - If no, what stops you from doing that?
2. How did you hear about Jesus?
3. Who is one person you could share Jesus with this week?

LIFE APPLICATION

SAY: Most of the time, when we have exciting news, we can't keep it to ourselves. We want everyone to know! The fact that Jesus died for you because he loves you is the most exciting news we can ever tell.

Wrap It Up

SAY: Who can you share Jesus with? Think of sharing your story, things like what Jesus did for you and what he means to you. Don't worry about having all of the answers. Just share from your heart. And if you feel afraid, ask God to give you boldness to share the greatest news ever!

Chapter 40: Back and Forth

Scripture: "Try your best to live in peace with everyone." – Hebrews 12:14

Topic
Sibling Rivalry

Purpose
To demonstrate how conflict goes back and forth between siblings.

Type:
Kid-volunteer

Supplies:
• Balloon, inflated

Preparation
Blow up the balloon ahead of time and tie it off.

PRESENTATION

SAY: How many of you have brothers or sisters? *(Allow answers)* What is the best thing about having a brother or sister? *(Allow answers)* What are some challenging things about having a brother or sister? *(Allow answers)* The relationship between brothers and sisters can be really great. You can play together, hang out together and make great memories. The relationship between brothers and sisters can also be tough sometimes. Sometimes, you fight and don't get along. Let me demonstrate this.

STEP 1: Invite 2 children to come to the front of the group.

SAY: I am going to toss a balloon out. It is your job to toss the balloon back and forth and keep it from hitting the floor. *(As the balloon is tossed from one side to the other, imitate a back-and-forth conversation that siblings might have.)*

Take It Further
Connect this object lesson to other Bible passages:
- Cain and Abel (Genesis 4)
- Jacob and Esau (Genesis 25:19-34)
- Mary and Martha (Luke 10:38-42)

"You get on my nerves." ---> "Yeah, well, you get on my nerves more."

"Stop taking my toys!" ---> "I can do whatever I want!"

"I'm telling Mom!" ---> "Go ahead, tell her. I don't care!"

"Get out of my room!" ---> "You're not the boss of me!"

Can you relate to any of that? It looks a bit silly, doesn't it? Sibling fights can go back and forth just like that poor balloon. There will be times we don't agree with other people. We need to learn how to solve them the right way.

STEP 2: Read Hebrews 12:14.

SAY: God calls us to find ways to live peacefully with each other. God gave us family relationships to teach us how to live in community with other people. Family relationships teach us how to love one another, forgive one another, share what we have, listen to each other and work together. If we spend more time doing all of that, we can possibly have less fighting and more loving. I'm pretty sure your parents would love that!

DISCUSSION QUESTIONS

1. Is there conflict in your relationship with a brother or sister?

2. How might the situation look different if you chose to handle it in a better way?

3. What is one way you can make peace with a brother or sister this week?

LIFE APPLICATION

SAY: We have to get along with our siblings. It would make our parents happy, but even more, it would make God happy. He wants us to live at peace with everyone.

Wrap It Up

SAY: Think about your relationship with your brothers or sisters. Are you a fight-starter or are you more of a peacemaker? Conflict is not always avoidable but you can work to find a peaceful solution instead of keeping the fight going.

Chapter 41: Uh-Oh

Scripture: "For all have sinned and fall short of the glory of God." – Romans 3:23, NIV

Topic
Sin

Purpose
To demonstrate how although our sins are many, we can be forgiven.

Type:
Science

Supplies:
- Clean sand
- Bucket or spray bottle with clean water
- Towel

Preparation
Place the sand on a tray or cookie sheet. Have a bucket or spray bottle of clean water and towel nearby.

PRESENTATION

SAY: I love going to the beach! Do you? *(Allow answers).* There are the waves, the surf, and the amazing sunsets. And let's not forget the sand. Sand is amazing.

STEP 1: Scoop some of the sand in your hand and walk around to allow the children to see it.

SAY: Have you ever looked closely at sand? How many grains of sand do you think I'm holding? *(Allow answers)* I can't be sure, but I bet there are at least *(come up with a number)* grains of sand in my hand right now.

After a day at the beach, you probably leave with sand in your hair, sand in your beach bag, and sand in your shoes! Sand is everywhere and in all of our stuff. We have to keep shaking everything out to get all of the sand out. Sin is a lot like that. It's in us; it's in everyone.

What is sin? *(Allow answers)* Sin can be defined as things we do that make God unhappy.

Take It Further

Connect this object lesson to other Bible passages:
- Sin Removed (Psalm 103:12)
- White as Snow (Isaiah 1:18)
- If You Know It, Do It (James 4:17)

Object Lesson:
Sin

STEP 2: Let the sand run between your fingers back in to the bucket as you talk.

SAY: Just like these grains of sand, sin can get into every nook and cranny of our lives. No matter how much we try to shake it off, sin will always be part of our lives. But thankfully, Jesus came   to help rescue us.

STEP 3: Read Romans 3:23.

SAY: God reminds us that we all sin. We are all guilty and this separates us from God.

STEP 4: Get out the spray bottle and towel.

SAY: No matter how much wrong we've done or how bad we think we are, Jesus loves us and forgives us. The Bible tells us he washes us clean, as white as snow (use the water to cleanse the sand from your hands), when we ask for forgiveness. We have to be willing to accept this gift. Did you receive that gift?

DISCUSSION QUESTIONS

1. Have you received Jesus as your Savior?

2. When you sin, do you ask God for forgiveness?

3. Do you think that God forgives some of your sin or all of your sin?

LIFE APPLICATION

SAY: No matter what we've done, we can be forgiven. That's why Jesus came. He loves us so much that he wanted to rescue us from our sin so that we can live with him forever.

Wrap It Up

SAY: Sin, like sand, invades everything. It separates us from God. Jesus created a way to get back to a relationship with God. We can be clean of our sin when we accept Christ into our hearts.

Chapter 42: Tug of Strength

Scripture: "But the Lord is faithful. He will strengthen you. He will guard you from the evil one."
— 2 Thessalonians 3:3

Topic
Strength

Purpose
To illustrate that no matter what we face, God gives us strength.

Type:
Kid-volunteer

Supplies:
- Light weights,
- Fitness ball,
- Jump rope or other exercise equipment (optional)
- Long, sturdy rope

Preparation
Plan on doing this activity in a large open space or outdoors.

PRESENTATION

STEP 1: Walk up front flexing your muscles.

SAY: My muscles help me do some amazing things, like lifting heavy things, running or jogging. I like to give my muscles a good workout by exercising. This helps me to build my strength. *(Use the optional exercise equipment here if you choose.)*

STEP 2: Read 2 Thessalonians 3:3.

SAY: This tells us that we can count on God to keep us strong. Sometimes it feels like we are in a tug of war with making the right decisions each day.

STEP 2: Play the traditional game of tug-of-war in an open area or outdoor space.

Take It Further

Connect this object lesson to other Bible passages:
- I Can Do All Things (Philippians 4:13)
- Strength to the Weary (Isaiah 40:29)
- Be Strong in the Lord (Ephesians 6:10)

Object Lesson:
Strength

SAY: Our inner strength is given to us by God so that when we face tough times, we can rely on him. There are times when God tells us what to do and there are other times when only God can do something in us. Only he can get the credit for those moments. That's what he wants us to do. He wants us to realize that when we're at the end of our rope *(just like our game)*, he can give us the strength to endure.

DISCUSSION QUESTIONS

1. What tough situation are you facing right now?
2. Is that situation too tough for God to help you?
3. What is one way that you can rely on God for strength right now?

LIFE APPLICATION

SAY: God wants us to condition our bodies to be strong and healthy, but he also wants us to allow him to condition us on the inside so that his strength can be in us.

Wrap It Up

SAY: Do you feel like there's a tough situation you can't face? There is nothing too hard for God. If you trust your situation to him, he can give you the strength to come out a winner. Sometimes things go differently than we plan but God's strength will help us come out on top!

Chapter 43: Go, Team, Go!

Scripture: "Two people are better than one. They can help each other in everything they do."
– Ecclesiastes 4:9

Topic
Teamwork

Purpose
To demonstrate that we can accomplish more when we work together.

Type:
Kid Volunteer

Supplies:
- 25 sturdy large plastic cups
- Tray like a cookie sheet

Preparation
- Set a single cup on the floor where you are teaching
- Set 24 cups close to each other in a rectangle and place the tray on top.

PRESENTATION

SAY: How many of you play a sport? *(Show of hands)* Let's say you show up the day of the game and you are the only one from your team there. Would you go out on the field or court alone? Why? *(Allow answers)* Well sure you wouldn't, you would get creamed!

STEP 1: Ask for a volunteer to come up.

SAY: I have a cup here. We are going to pretend this cup is a person. This person's task is to hold up *(fill in name of volunteer)*. I want you to stand on the cup for a few seconds and step down. This action will represent something that this person (point to the cup) has to do. *(The child will step up on the cup and it will crush.)* What happened? By itself, it was not able to accomplish the task.

STEP 2: Walk the child over to where you have the 24 cups and the tray.

SAY: Okay here I have a group of people trying to accomplish the same task together. Step up on the tray.

Take It Further

Connect this object lesson to other Bible passages:
- I Can Do All Things (Philippians 4:13)
- Strength to the Weary (Isaiah 40:29)
- Be Strong in the Lord (Ephesians 6:10)

Object Lesson:
Teamwork

STEP 3: Allow the child to step up on the tray, remain for a few seconds and step down.

SAY: What happened? *(Allow answers)* That's right, together the cups/people were able to accomplish the task of holding up the pressure of the person. *(Thank the child and have them sit down.)*

STEP 4: Read Ecclesiastes 4:9.

SAY: God designed us to work together and not try and get things done alone. That is one of the main reasons the church comes together. You know you are with others trying to follow Christ.

Let me give you an example. You are at school and someone is picking on another child. Everyone is watching, but no one is trying to help that child. You think you should do something, but you look around and see that no one else is doing anything. What goes through your mind? *(Allow answers)* What if all of a sudden several kids spoke up at once and told that bully to stop. Would you feel braver stepping into that situation then? *(Allow answers)* Sure you would. Because you are not alone. Should you still be courageous in this situation and do what is right even if you are the only one? Absolutely, and God would be with you in that, but the point is when we band together, we feel stronger and difficult things are not overwhelming.

DISCUSSION QUESTIONS

1. Do you ask for help when you need it?
  - If not, what stops you from doing that?

2. Where do you find friends that will stand with you?

3. Who can you ask to stand with you and help you?

LIFE APPLICATION

SAY: We can accomplish more when we work together. Surround yourself with friends that will stand with you and help you in tasks and challenges.

Wrap It Up

SAY: These cups *(point to the cups and tray)* worked together to get the job done. We can accomplish so much more when we join forces with other Christians to encourage and help each other.

Chapter 44: Sweet Words, Sour Words

Scripture: "Don't let any evil talk come out of your mouths. Say only what will help to build others up and meet their needs. Then what you say will help those who listen." – Ephesians 4:29

Topic
Tongue/Words

Purpose
To help children realize the power their words have on others.

Type:
Food,
Kid Volunteer

Supplies:
- Sweet candy
- Sour candy
- Index cards
- Pens/pencils/markers

Preparation

Ahead of time, put the index cards in stacks of 10-12.

PRESENTATION

SAY: The words that we speak have tremendous power. They have the ability to build someone up (or be sweet) or the ability to tear someone down (or be sour). *(Give an example of how words can be used to build up and tear down.)*

STEP 1: Divide the children into groups of 5 or 6. Give them each a stack of the index cards and something to write with.

SAY: Brainstorm 5 – 6 words or phrases that might build someone up and write each word or phrase on the index cards. Then brainstorm 5 – 6 words or phrases that might tear someone down and write each word or phrase on the remaining index cards.

STEP 2: Collect the index cards from each group and shuffle them. Distribute a handful of each type of candy to each child. Tell them not to eat the candy yet. Be ready to read the cards, one at a time.

Take It Further

Connect this object lesson to other Bible passages:
- Be Careful About What You Say (Proverbs 21:23)
- Tongue of the Wise (Proverbs 12:18)
- Tongue Guard (Psalm 141:3)

Object Lesson:
Tongue/Words

(Tip: Limit the number of cards you read. You don't want them eating too much candy.)

SAY: As I read these cards. If you hear a word or phrase that would build someone up, eat a sweet piece of candy. If I read a word or phrase that might tear someone down, eat a sour piece of candy. *(Read through the cards)*

What reaction did your mouth have when you had the sweet and then sour candy? *(Allow answers)* That is the same way it feels to someone who is receiving your words. Your words have a lot of power.

STEP 3: Read Ephesians 4:29.

SAY: Our verse today says that God calls us to build each other up. Has anyone ever heard someone say, "If you can't say something nice, say nothing at all."? This is a good practice to get into. We often think things about people, but if it isn't a good thing we shouldn't say anything.

DISCUSSION QUESTIONS

1. How did the sweet candy make your mouth feel?
2. How did the sour candy make your mouth feel?
3. How might the words we use have those same effects on those who hear our words?

LIFE APPLICATION

SAY: The words that we speak have the ability to make someone feel good or bad. If we're not careful, the words we speak can cause hurt and pain.

Wrap It Up

SAY: I would hope that no one here hurts someone's feelings on purpose. I pray that if we do speak words that hurt, it would be by mistake. Sometimes being frustrated, angry, or in a hurry can cause us to not be careful with our words, but if we take the time to think about what we're saying, it could save us from having to use our tongues to say, "I'm sorry for saying that."

Chapter 45: Blind Trust

Scripture: "Lord, those who know you will trust in you. You have never deserted those who look to you."
– Psalm 9:10, NIRV

Topic
Trust

Purpose
To demonstrate how things that obstruct our view can cause us not to trust what's unseen.

Type:
Everyday objects

Supplies:
- Blindfold
- Sunglasses
- Hat with a visor
- Fog machine and fog juice (optional)

Preparation
Set up the materials where they are easily accessed from the presentation area.

Note
If using the fog machine and fog juice, prepare according to machine instructions.

PRESENTATION

SAY: I think I have pretty good vision. *(Add if you wear glasses or contacts: when I use my glasses or wear my contacts)* I can see everything pretty clearly as I walk, ride my bicycle, and drive my car. However, sometimes, I can't see as clearly. Sometimes, when I'm out and about in my day, there are things that get in the way of my ability to see clearly.

STEP 1: Put on the blindfold.

SAY: When you're at a birthday party, you might play pin-the-tail on the donkey or take a few swings at a piñata. You might not be able to see clearly but you need a blindfold to play fairly.

STEP 2: Take off the blindfold and put on the sunglasses.

SAY: Sometimes, the glare from the sun is just so bright it blinds my eyes. These sunglasses allow me to see better on sunny days, but it can make things a bit darker.

STEP 3: Take off the sunglasses and put on the hat with a visor.

SAY: I love my caps,

Take It Further

Connect this object lesson to other Bible passages:
- God Can Be Trusted (2 Samuel 7:28)
- Trust in God (Proverbs 3:5-6)
- Faith Unseen (Hebrews 11:1)

especially ones that have a logo of my favorite sports team! If I wear the cap way down over my eyes *(pull the cap down over your eyes a bit)*, I can't see some of the things around me.

STEP 4: Turn on the fog machine. *(Omit this step if you are not using the fog machine)*

SAY: When we drive, fog can be so thick it's hard to see directly in front of you. That can be scary. Seeing helps us trust our next move.

STEP 5: Read Psalm 9:10.

SAY: We cannot see God. Sometimes that causes us to hesitate to trust him with our next step. However, God is trustworthy. For thousands of years he has kept all his promises to us and kept us safe. We can trust him even if we can't see everything he is doing.

DISCUSSION QUESTIONS

1. Is it harder for you to trust what you see or don't see?

2. How does that affect the way you trust God?

3. Is it hard to trust in a God you can't see?

LIFE APPLICATION

SAY: It's very easy for us to trust what we see but it takes faith and courage to trust what we can't see.

Wrap It Up

SAY: Even though we can't see him, God wants us to trust him wholeheartedly. He wants us to have the faith to believe that he is who he says he is and he'll do what he says he'll do. Do you trust him?

Chapter 46: Beyond a Shadow of a Doubt

Scripture: "Here is what I am commanding you to do. Be strong and brave. Do not be terrified. Do not lose hope. I am the Lord your God. I will be with you everywhere you go."
– Joshua 1:9

Topic
Uncertainty/ Doubt

Type:
Kid-involved

Supplies:
- Chair

Preparation
None

Purpose
To help children feel comforted knowing that it's okay if they have questions about things they're not sure about.

PRESENTATION

STEP 1: Stand behind a chair.

SAY: I need a volunteer. *(Allow someone to come up – make it someone small)* I have here a chair. How many of you came in and sat down without checking the chair first to make sure it was strong enough to hold you? *(Show of hands-should be everyone)* Why didn't you check it? *(Allow answers)* Hmm, seems like you do things every day that show your trust and faith. *(Drive in a car, place your plate on a table, get in an elevator, etc.)* You have had enough experiences to realize that you probably don't need to doubt the chair will hold you to the point where you don't even think about it anymore.

STEP 2: Invite the child to sit in the chair.

SAY: (Child's name), have a seat. *(Child should sit down without concern).* I want to try a test today. I am going to lean this chair back with you in it.

Take It Further

Connect this object lesson to other Bible passages:
- Doubting Thomas (John 20:24-29)
- Jesus Calms the Storm (Matthew 8:23-27)
- Jesus Heals a Boy Possessed By an Impure Spirit (Mark 9:14-29)

Object Lesson:
Uncertainty/Doubt

(Start to lean the chair back more and more until it feels a bit uneasy for the child. Wobble it a bit and then bring the chair back to the floor)

Wow, you let me lean you back pretty far. Were you afraid I was going to drop you? *(Allow answer)* (Child's name) trusted me to keep him/her safe.

STEP 3: Read Joshua 1:9.

SAY: God is reminding us that no matter where we go or what we do we can count on him to be with us. We need to remember he is with us always. This should help us to feel strong and brave. To have courage. We can trust God to take care of us.

DISCUSSION QUESTIONS

1. Do you ever doubt God is with you?

2. How can you help yourself remember he is with you?

LIFE APPLICATION

SAY: It's a very brave thing to ask questions when we don't know the answer or when we struggle to believe what we might not understand. That's ok. God wants us to come to him with all of our questions so that he can lead us to the truth.

Wrap It Up

SAY: God understands that we have a hard time believing things we can't see or control. That is how we grow our faith. God is trustworthy. We can count on him to help us and teach us.

Chapter 47: Out Comes Wisdom

Scripture: "If any of you needs wisdom, ask God for it. He will give it to you. God gives freely to everyone. He doesn't find fault." – James 1:5

Topic
Wisdom

Purpose
To empower children to ask God to give them wisdom.

Type:
Everyday Objects
Kid Volunteer

Supplies:
- Large dry sponge
- Squirt gun (any size)
- Bowl to squeeze water into

Preparation
Fill the squirt gun ahead of time. Place all the supplies on a table by where you will teach.

PRESENTATION

SAY: How many of you know that wisdom and knowledge are not the same thing? Knowledge is when we learn. We can learn Bible stories, memorize scripture, learn right from wrong. That is what we know.

STEP 1: Hold up the large dry sponge.

  SAY: Let's pretend this sponge is each of you. When you learn it is like this squirter is sending in the knowledge to your brain.

STEP 2: Ask for a volunteer to hold out the sponge at arms length. Take aim and squirt the sponge. Play a bit here. Kids love to laugh and it helps them remember. You can pretend to accidentally squirt the volunteer.

  SAY: I am filling the sponge up with water. It is in there to come out when it is needed. *(Thank the volunteer and take the sponge. Have the volunteer sit down.)* If this sponge is us, and we have

Take It Further

Connect this object lesson to other Bible passages:
- Speak Words of Wisdom (Psalm 37:30)
- Stay Close to Wisdom (Proverbs 4:6-7)
- Heavenly Wisdom (James 3:17)

gone to school and church and learned, or listened to our parents and learned, then we are filled with knowledge.

STEP 3: Hold the sponge over the bowl.

SAY: Wisdom is being able to take that knowledge and use it well. So when the knowledge comes out of us *(squeeze the sponge into the bowl)* that shows how much wisdom we have. You can be really smart and still make dumb decisions, because you lack wisdom, or the ability to use that knowledge in a good way.

STEP 4: Read James 1:5.

SAY: God promises to help us be wise. He says in this verse that we only have to ask him for help. How do we ask God for help? *(Allow answers)* That's right, we pray. First we have to stop before we make a decision, then pray. It is harder to undo a bad action or choice after you have done it. Stop and pray first and God will help you see what you need to do.

DISCUSSION QUESTIONS

1. What does it mean to be wise?

2. What does this Bible verse say we should do to become wise?

3. What is the first thing you should do when you have to make a decision?

LIFE APPLICATION

SAY: Many people can be smart, but being wise is different. It means looking at a situation and using good judgment to make a decision. It's not always easy but we can all be wise. How? By asking God for help.

Wrap It Up

SAY: All of us can be wise people by asking God to give us wisdom. The wisdom that he gives will help us to know what to do in tough situations and help us know how to be more like him.

Chapter 48: To the Finish Line

Scripture: "Work at everything you do with all your heart. Work as if you were working for the Lord, not for human masters." – Colossians 3:23

Purpose
To illustrate how important it is to finish what you start.

Type:
Everyday objects

Supplies:
- Copy of a chore chart
- Video game controller
- Book
- Sports ball (any kind will work)
- Small piece of fruit

Preparation

Set the supplies on a table in the front of your presentation area.

Tip: Make a chore chart if you don't have one. Make a 5 column grid with names across the top and chores down the side. Put a few stickers or check marks in different columns.

PRESENTATION

STEP 1: Hold up a chore chart.

SAY: How many of you do chores at home? Many kids your age do chores at home. You probably won't believe me, but most parents don't have their children do chores just to do the chores. Parents want you to grow up and be responsible adults, so they give you chores as a young person to help you get into the habit of pitching in and taking care of your things.

I don't really know of many kids who enjoy doing chores. In fact, I don't know many grown-ups who enjoy doing chores.

Think about your attitude when you do your chores or when you're asked to do your chores. Do you complain and say things like, "But Mom..." or "Gee Dad, I was getting ready to..."?

STEP 2: Get behind the other objects and prepare to hold them up.
SAY: Maybe you get so wrapped up in what you are doing you don't want to stop, like:

Take It Further

Connect this object lesson to other Bible passages:
- Commit to the Lord (Proverbs 16:3)
- For the Glory of God (1 Corinthians 10:31)
- Work With All Your Might (Ecclesiastes 9:10)

- playing video games *(manipulate the controller)*?
- reading a book *(pretend to read the book)*?
- playing ball *(toss or kick the ball as appropriate)*? or
- eating a snack *(eat some of the snack)*?

It is okay to enjoy things. But what would happen if we never did our chores? What if Mom never got groceries? Or Dad never put gas in the car? What if Mom or Dad didn't go to work? What would happen if the trash wasn't taken out ever? We all do our part to get things done. We have to get into the habit of doing our part right away. God is pleased with us when we do our part. Our verse says to do our chores like we are doing them for God.

STEP 3: Read Colossians 3:23.

SAY: So what can we do? Learn what God wants us to do by reading the Bible and talking to him.

DISCUSSION QUESTIONS

1. Are you one who does chores right away or puts it off until the last minute?
2. Why do you think you do that?
3. How might your attitude toward doing tasks change if you think about doing it for God and not the grown up at your house?

LIFE APPLICATION

SAY: When you start a project or are responsible for a task, you don't just want to finish it. You want to finish it well.

Wrap It Up

SAY: When we are given a job to do, we can honor God with by doing it with a good attitude (not complaining or mumbling) and a determination to finish what we start.

Top 50 Object Lessons: Games & Activities

Chapter 49: Not Weighed Down

Scripture: Turn all your worries over to him. He cares about you. – 1 Peter 5:7

Topic
Worry/Anxiety

Purpose
To demonstrate how heavy our burdens are when we're filled with worry.

Type:
Everyday objects
Kid Volunteer

Supplies:
- 1 or 2 water pails or buckets
- 2 or 4 sponges
- Towels (for any spills)

Preparation

Fill the pails or buckets with a small amount of water. Place a sponge in each of the water pails so that the sponges absorb the water. Place the remaining supplies on a table in front of your presentation area.

PRESENTATION

SAY: Today, we're going to talk about worry and how it affects us. What does it mean to worry? (*Allow answers.*) Yes! Worry is when we focus on how things will turn out. Sometimes we worry about things that we can control and sometimes we worry about things beyond our control.

When we worry about things, we can sometimes be weighed down. It can make us feel like we're carrying a ton of bricks.

STEP 1: Invite one or two children up to the front of the presentation area. Have them stand behind or near the pails or buckets of water. Give them a dry sponge to hold.

SAY: How heavy does this sponge feel? (*Allow answer.*) (*The dry sponge should not feel heavy at all.*)

STEP 2: Then have the children pick up (*but not wring out*) the sponge inside of the pail.

Take It Further

Connect this object lesson to other Bible passages:
- Don't Worry (Philippians 4:6-7)
- No Troubled Hearts (John 14:27)
- I'm Afraid (Psalm 56:3)

 Top 50 Object Lessons: Games & Activities

SAY: Which sponge was heavier? *(They should respond that the wet sponge is heavier.)* So the sponge with the water is heavier than the dry sponge. Worry is a lot like the wet sponges. Worry can sometimes fill every nook and cranny until we are weighed down. When we've reached our fill, our stomachs can get all twisted *(invite the volunteers to wring out the sponges into the pails)* until we feel like we have nothing left.

STEP 3: Read 1 Peter 5:7.

SAY: This verse reminds us that we are to hand all our worries to God and he will take care of them for us.

DISCUSSION QUESTIONS

1. Is there something that you're worried about today?
2. How does worrying about something affect you?
3. What does 1 Peter 5:7 tell us we should do instead of worrying?

LIFE APPLICATION

SAY: Life is filled with so many twists and turns and ups and downs. It's easy to get overwhelmed with things and worry sometimes. But God doesn't want us to worry. He wants us to trade our worry for his peace.

Wrap It Up

SAY: Letting go of our worries will free us to experience God's peace. He cares about us and doesn't want us to carry burdens around. He wants to carry them for us. Will you let him?

Chapter 50: Whole Heart Worship

Scripture: *"...I will praise the LORD with all my heart."* – Psalm 111:1

Topic
Worship

Purpose
To illustrate how God wants our whole heart when we worship him.

Type:
Everyday objects

Supplies:
- Large red piece of paper or poster board
- Scissors
- Black marker
- Painter's tape

Preparation

Cut a large heart from the paper or poster board. Then cut the poster board heart into 3 large pieces. Label the 3 pieces as follows:
- "FOCUS"
- "LOVE"
- "PRAISE"

Set the heart pieces and marker to the side in the front of your presentation area.

PRESENTATION

SAY: I love to sing! My favorite song is *(insert name of your favorite Christian worship song)*. Singing that song really helps me to worship Jesus and focus on who he is. Do you have a favorite song that helps you focus on Jesus? *(Allow answers)* Music is very powerful, but music isn't all there is to worship. There are 3 parts of worship that I want to share with you:

STEP 1: Hold up the 'Focus' piece of the cut out heart.

SAY: When we are worshipping God we are focusing on him. *(Tape up the 'Focus' piece on the wall to begin creating the large heart.)*

STEP 2: Hold up the 'Love' piece.

SAY: Love - When we worship God, we show him that we love him. We love him because he first loved us and gave his son Jesus as a sacrifice for us. We give offerings and we bring a heart that is ready to hear what he has to say to us. *(Tape the 'Love' piece to its spot.)*

Take It Further

Connect this object lesson to other Bible passages:
- God is Worthy of Our Praise (Psalm 29)
- He Alone is God (Psalm 86:9-10)
- Shout for Joy (Psalm 100)

Object Lesson:
Worship

STEP 3: Hold up the 'Praise' piece of the heart.

SAY: Praise - When we praise God, it means that we tell him how grateful we are for him and what he's done for us. We thank him for our blessings and ask him to help us love him even more. *(Tape this last piece on the wall to complete the large heart.)* When all three of these are part of our time with God, we are truly worshipping with our whole heart.

STEP 4: Read Psalm 111:1.

SAY: We now know that worship is more than just singing. It is focusing on God, showing him our love and giving him the praise he deserves. Is that all happening when you worship? Is singing the only way to worship? *(Allow answers)* No, when we serve God, pray, and thoughtfully read the Bible, we are worshipping God too.

DISCUSSION QUESTIONS

1. Would you say that you love God with all of your heart?

2. Read Psalm 111:1. Would you say that you praise God with all your heart?

3. What might stop you from worshipping God fully?

LIFE APPLICATION

SAY: Giving God our focus, love, and praise are ways to worship him with all of our hearts. We give him our all because he gave us his all.

Wrap It Up

SAY: Worship is more than music. It's the content of our hearts. It's the words we say, the words we don't say, and the spirit in which we prepare to worship. You can worship God with all of your heart because he loves you with all of his.

Chapter 51: Filled with Purpose

Scripture: "God made us. He created us to belong to Christ Jesus. Now we can do good things. Long ago God prepared them for us to do."
– Ephesians 2:10

Topic
Purpose

Purpose
To illustrate how God fills us with purpose so that we can live for him.

Type:
Everyday Objects Games

Supplies:
- Drinking cup
- Measuring cup
- Latex balloon (keep a few extra on hand just in case)

Preparation
None.

PRESENTATION

SAY: Every day, we use things that were created for special purposes. For instance, look at this cup.

STEP 1: Hold up the drinking cup.

   SAY: What is this cup designed for? *(Allow answers)* That's right. A cup like this one is designed for us to drink liquid like water, juice, or milk from. Now, what is this cup designed for?

STEP 2: Hold up the measuring cup.

   SAY: That's right. This is a cup, too, but this cup helps us measure things like flour and sugar. It helps us make sure we don't add too much to a recipe when we're cooking. We looked at two different cups, both designed with a special purpose. We are also designed with a special purpose. Each of us is God's creation, created for a purpose.

STEP 3: Read Ephesians 4:10.

   SAY: God made each of us with different gifts, talents, and passions but he wants all of us to use what he

Take It Further

Connect this object lesson to other Bible passages:
- Gifts of the Holy Spirit (1 Corinthians 12)
- Made in His Image (Genesis 1:26-27)
- Parable of the Talents (Matthew 25:14-30)

gives us for one common goal – to bring glory to him. Just like this balloon needs air put into it to fulfill its purpose.

STEP 4: Inflate the balloon by mouth and holding it to keep the air in.

SAY: God breathes his life into us to fulfill our purpose. Then, we're able to use what he's given us to do what he wants us to do. It is important to ask God what he has designed you for. As you explore your unique gifts and interests, God will reveal your purpose for him.

DISCUSSION QUESTIONS

1. What are some things you like to do?

2. What are things that you do well?

3. How can you use those gifts/talents to glorify God?

LIFE APPLICATION

SAY: We are all uniquely created by God for a purpose. We might not be good at everything but there's one thing we can all do. Use what God has given you to make the world a better place for him!

Wrap It Up

Hold up the inflated balloon and tie it to keep the air in. **SAY:** God has breathed life into all of us and he wants us to use our gifts and talents to bring him glory. When we do that, we are free to soar high *(toss balloon up into the air and keep it bouncing while you talk)* and share our gifts with the world!

Chapter 52: The Gift of Grace

Scripture: *"For it is by grace you have been saved, through faith—and this is not from yourselves, it is the gift of God—not by works, so that no one can boast."*
– Ephesians 2:8-9, NIV

**Topic
Grace**

Purpose

To help children understand that we are all winners in God's eyes because of his grace.

Type:
Games

Supplies:

- Variety of balls - tennis ball, basketball, football, baseball, etc

Preparation

None

PRESENTATION

SAY: How many of you are on a sports team where balls are part of the game? *(Allow answers).* There are lots of reasons why kids your age are on sports teams. While there are many different reasons for why we play and many different kinds of sports games to play, games that involve balls have one theme - to use the ball to help us win!

STEP 1: Hold up the football.

> **SAY:** Sometimes, you have to get the ball from one end of the field to the next.

STEP 2: Hold up the baseball.

> **SAY:** Sometimes, you have to get the ball to the bat so you can hit it and run bases.

STEP 3: Hold up the basketball.

> **SAY:** Sometimes, you have to aim and shoot the ball so that it goes through the net.

Take It Further

Connect this object lesson to other Bible passages:
- Boast the Right Way (Jeremiah 9:23-24)
- Grace, Grace, Grace (Romans 11:6)
- God's Grace in Me (1 Corinthians 15:10)

 Top 50 Object Lessons: Games & Activities

Object Lesson: Grace

Hitting these types of goals usually involve some kind of game where there is a winner and a loser. We like to win but let's talk about losing for a minute. We have all experienced being the loser at some point. Either in a sport or maybe failing a test, not having someone like you, etc. When you are in that moment, it is hard. You don't want someone to make you feel worse. If they are the winner, you want them to be gracious and kind to you. That is what God has done. Because of our sin we had all lost our connection with God. We were all losers. God showed love and kindness to us by offering us the gift of grace and forgiveness. He made it possible for us to all be winners.

STEP 4: Read Ephesians 2:8-9.

SAY: God gave us the best example of graciousness when he sent his Son, Jesus, so that we can have salvation.

DISCUSSION QUESTIONS

1. Who here has ever lost something?
2. Who has won?
3. How does it feel that God loves you and wanted to be close to you?

LIFE APPLICATION

SAY: In God's eyes, there are no losers. We're all winners because of his gift of grace to us. His gift isn't given to us because we earn it or even deserve it but because of his great love for us.

Wrap It Up

SAY: No one plays a game with the intention of losing. We all practice and play with the hopes of winning, right? In those moments, though, when we lose, we can remember that in God's eyes we are all winners. He sees us through the gift of grace.

Chapter 53: Building Community

Scripture: "And let us not give up meeting together. Some are in the habit of doing this. Instead, let us cheer each other up with words of hope. Let us do it all the more as you see the day coming when Christ will return."

– Hebrews 10:25

Topic Community

Purpose
To illustrate the importance of living in community.

Type:
Game

Supplies:
- 4-in-a-row game
- Tape
- Permanent marker

Preparation
Put the tape on 4 disks and write the words:
- Busy
- Sports
- Lazy,
- Activities

PRESENTATION

STEP 1: Have the 4-in-a Row game on the table in front of you. *(During this step: As you talk, begin to drop your color disks down the chute trying to get 4 in a row. Pause before you make 4-in-a-row. As you talk, have a volunteer adult sneak in and block you with their color disk. Have fun with it. Start to talk and be surprised when your stealth partner sneaks in and stops you.)*

SAY: I have up here a game many of you have seen before. The goal of the game is to get all four disks the same color in a row together. It is pretty easy. Let's pretend that each of these disks are people in my church, friends and family, my community. I want to be together with them.

STEP 2: Drop in a disk and look to the side. While you are looking away, your covert partner drops the **BUSY** disk in next to yours and hides behind you. Notice the new disk and be surprised.

SAY: Wait, where did that come from? What does it say? It says **BUSY** on it. Oh well, I'll go this way.

Take It Further

Connect this object lesson to other Bible passages:
- Sharing Life Together (Acts 2:42-47)
- Bear One Another's Burdens (Galatians 6:2)
- One Body, Many Parts (1 Corinthians 12:25-27)

Object Lesson: Community

Instead of trying to be in control of things and people, our goal should be to follow God's lead. He is the one in control and knows what's best. He wants to be in control of the plans you make, the words you say, the things you do, and the places you go. Why? Because he wants what is best for you.

STEP 3: Drop in another. Turn and look away, your partner sneaks in again and drops the **SPORTS** disk to block you. Notice the disk.

SAY: Hey, now where did this one come from. What does it say? **SPORTS**, Hmm weird.

STEP 4: Continue this with **LAZY** and **ACTIVITIES.**

SAY: Man there always seems to be things that can get in the way of me being with my church community, and friends. But I am going to keep trying because it is important to me. *(Continue to drop in your disks and block your opponent. Get your 4-in-a-row.)* Being with my community is important to me. I will do what I have to not let anything stop me.

STEP 5: Read Hebrews 10:25.

SAY: God wants us to come together regularly to encourage each other. We have to make the effort to not let other things get in the way of this.

DISCUSSION QUESTIONS

1. Is attending church regularly important to you and your family?
2. What are some things that get in your way to come to church?
3. How have you connected with people you attend church with?

LIFE APPLICATION

SAY: God does not want us to go through life alone. He wants us to build meaningful connections with others through community.

Wrap It Up

SAY: We build community with others by building relationships with others and supporting each other when we can. Be on the lookout for things that get in the way of you going to church and stop them from being the obstacle.

Chapter 54: The Hand You Were Dealt

Scripture: "For I know the plans I have for you," declares the LORD, "plans to prosper you and not to harm you, plans to give you hope and a future." – Jeremiah 29:11, NIV

Topic
Uncertainty

Purpose
To demonstrate how to handle uncertainty that comes our way.

Type:
Games
Action

Supplies:
- Deck of cards (any variety you'd like)

Preparation
None.

PRESENTATION

SAY: When you play a card game with a friend, you usually shuffle and deal out a certain number of cards. You don't know what cards you're going to get. You get what you get! Let's see what happens.

STEP 1: Take the deck of cards, hold them up in the air, arch them really hard and let them go. They should fly all over the place. Typically, kids get so excited about this that they rush to grab them. Let that happen. If it doesn't tell them to grab whatever cards they find.

STEP 2: Bring their attention back to you.

   SAY: Hold on to your cards. Separate out your red cards and your black. Which one do you have more of? Okay, everyone with more red cards come on this side, and everyone with more black cards over here. *(Decide what to do based on your space available.)*

STEP 3: Bring their attention back to you.

   SAY: You didn't have anything to do with the cards you got. They

Take It Further

Connect this object lesson to other Bible passages:
- Be Strong and Courageous (Deuteronomy 31:6)
- Never Alone (Hebrews 13:5)
- Always Thankful (1 Thessalonians 5:18)

came to you. Let's pretend the red cards are good things that happen *(like getting an A on a test, or a special trip),* and the black cards are difficult things that happen, *(like moving away from friends or not doing well on a test.)* Most everyone should have both black and red cards. Sometimes for those on this side *(point to the black side)* it may seem like too many difficult things happen. But God uses each challenge to make us strong and better. God sends us good things too to remind us of his love and grace.

STEP 4: Have everyone sit down and give you back the cards.

SAY: We may not know when good or difficult things will happen in our life, but we know God is in control of it all.

STEP 5: Read Jeremiah 29:11

SAY: God has planned out our life and will be with us each step of the way through the good and the bad. God does not waste any experiences. He allows them and uses them to help us grow closer to him. It can help during the tough times to look for the good things God has blessed us with.

DISCUSSION QUESTIONS

1. Have you ever had something unexpected (good or bad) happen to you?

2. How did you handle it?

3. How can you look for good when hard things happen?

LIFE APPLICATION

SAY: Life is full of uncertainties but we don't have to worry. Whatever God allows to happen is part of his plan for our lives.

Wrap It Up

SAY: Life can be full of wonderful, happy moments. Life can also be full of sad, unexpected moments. Either way, it's all in God's plan for us. No matter what hand you're dealt, you can be sure that God will be with you every step of the way.

Chapter 55: Get Back Up

Scripture: "So cheer each other up with the hope you have. Build each other up." – 1 Thessalonians 5:11

Topic
Endurance

Purpose
To help children understand that when someone falls down, they can help them back up.

Type:
Games
Science

Supplies:
- 2 sets of Dominoes
- Bible

Preparation
- Set up one set of dominos in a normal way.
- Set up a second set of dominos right up against each other, ending up against the Bible.

PRESENTATION

SAY: How many of you have ever fallen down? *(Allow answers).* You might even have a scar or two to remind you of when you've fallen. Do you have people in your life that will stand strong with you and help you be better?

STEP 1: Stand behind the table of set up dominos. Hold up a domino.

SAY: Look at these dominoes. We have people that we come across in our life all the time. Kids at school, and people in our neighborhood. Are they good people that do Godly things? Who are you deciding to hang out with? When someone does something they shouldn't it affects everyone around them. If these are not strong friends, they fall away from you when you mess up and aren't there to help you stand strong. Right now they are standing straight but one little push and down they'll go.

STEP 2: Knock down the dominos.

Take It Further

Connect this object lesson to other Bible passages:
- My Help Comes From the Lord (Psalm 121)
- The Good Samaritan (Luke 10:25-37)
- Friends Help Paralyzed Man (Mark 2:1-12)

SAY: See how there was not support to stand strong even if you make a mistake?

STEP 3: Stand behind the table with the dominos right next to each other and up against the Bible.

SAY: These dominos are supported by close friends. These are people in your life that you can count on to do what God wants. See they are backed up by the Bible. If you begin to make a mistake your close friends that love God are there to help you.

STEP 4: Set the domino in your hand at the end of this line of dominos. They should be right up against each other with the last domino up against the Bible.

SAY: The more friends and community I have around me the better my chance that someone will catch me before I make a mistake and stop me before it gets out of hand. *(Try knocking them down.)*

STEP 5: Read 1 Thessalonians 5:11.

SAY: God wants us to be in friendships where we are supported and helped. We are to encourage and build each other up.

DISCUSSION QUESTIONS

1. Can you recall a time when you've fallen down?
2. Was anyone there to help you?
3. Are you someone who helps someone when they're down? How do you help them?

LIFE APPLICATION

SAY: Being a good friend means being there to help our friends up when they fall down or feel down.

Wrap It Up

SAY: It's hard and painful to take a fall and it's hard and painful to watch someone else take a fall, too. If we are a good friend, we are there to take care of our friend and help them get back on their feet. Lending a helping hand is what a good friend does.

Chapter 56: My Yes Is My Yes

Scripture: "But what about you?" he asked. "Who do you say I am?" – Matthew 16:15, NIV

Topic
Assurance

Purpose
To help children understand what they believe and why.

Type:
Games
Kid Volunteer

Supplies:
- 2-3 toy hoops

Preparation
None

PRESENTATION

SAY: Some of the things you children play with are really simple. Take this toy, for instance. *(Hold up a toy hoop.)* This is a simple toy but it offers a lot of fun for people who know how to use it.

STEP 1: Call 2-3 children up to the front or center of the presentation area. Give each volunteer a toy hoop and instruct them to use the toy hoop to see who can do the most circles in 60 seconds. Encourage the other children to cheer on the volunteers.

SAY: What did you notice about these toy hoops as they were being used? *(Allow answers)* The toy hoops were going around in circles. They kept going around and around and around.

Sometimes, when we have to make a decision, we can go around and around in circles, just like these toy hoops. We run around to all our friends and ask them what they think. Sometimes we get so many different answers it's hard to know what decision to make.

Take It Further

Connect this object lesson to other Bible passages:
- Yes or No (Matthew 5:37)
- What Do You Believe (John 11:26)
- Jesus Heals a Demon-Possessed Boy (Mark 9:14-29)

Object Lesson:
Assurance

STEP 2: Hold up the Bible.

SAY: In God's Word, we learn about who Jesus is. He is the Son of God, our Savior, our friend.

The Bible tells us about a conversation Jesus had with Peter, one of his disciples. Jesus asked Peter a fairly simple question.

STEP 3: Read Matthew 16:15.

SAY: There had been a lot of talk about who Jesus was. Just like these toy hoops, they were going around and around with answers. Some said he was a prophet, a teacher, a rabbi, a really crazy person who thought he was God. Jesus wanted to know if Peter really believed who he was. Peter had seen all that Jesus had done. All the amazing words and miracles.

STEP 4: Hold up the Bible again and a toy hoop.

SAY: There will always be friends that tell you Jesus isn't real. We aren't supposed to run around listening to everyone else's opinion of who Jesus is. We know from God's Word he is our Savior and God. He is our friend and he loves us. He died for our sins so we can have a relationship with God.

DISCUSSION QUESTIONS

1. When you think about your relationship with Jesus, who do you say he is to you?
2. What do you believe about Jesus?
3. Why do you believe that?

LIFE APPLICATION

SAY: Most times, when we believe in something, we know why we believe in it. It's no different when we believe in Jesus. It's important to not only believe in him but understand what we believe and why we believe it.

Wrap It Up

SAY: When Jesus asked Peter who he says Jesus is, Peter answered him back with, "You are the Messiah, the Son of the living God." He didn't have to think about it. He knew it and wasn't afraid to say it. What about you? Do you know who Jesus is and why you believe in him?

Chapter 57: Jump for Joy

Scripture: *"A cheerful heart is good medicine..."*
– Proverbs 17:22, NIV

Topic
Joy

Type:

Games
Kid Volunteer

Supplies:

• Jump ropes

Preparation

None

Purpose

To demonstrate that true joy comes from God.

PRESENTATION

SAY: When we are sick and feeling yucky, what do we take to make us feel better? *(Allow answers).* That's right, we take medicine. Now, tell me what we take when feel sad? *(Allow answers).* That was a tricky question, wasn't it? Usually when we're sad, we don't take medicine. We usually do something that makes us happy, like play with a friend, watch our favorite movie, cuddle with our favorite teddy bear, or eat a yummy snack.

STEP 1: Read Proverbs 17.

SAY: This verse tells us that a cheerful heart is good medicine. Hmm, I wonder what that means. Do you have any ideas what that means? *(Allow answers).* A heart filled with joy is good for us. It's like medicine for our bodies when we're sick. It makes us feel better!

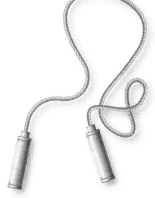

When we think about all of our blessings from God, it should make us scream and shout and jump for joy! Let's do that now. I need a few helpers to come and join me up front.

Take It Further

Connect this object lesson to other Bible passages:

- Joy of the Lord (Nehemiah 8:10)
- Filled With Joy (Romans 15:13)
- Praise the Lord (Psalm 150:6)

Object Lesson:
Joy

STEP 2: Invite a few volunteers to come up. Hand them a jump rope.

SAY: Think about things that make your heart happy. I want you to take one jump for each thing that makes their heart happy. Everyone count how many jumps are taken.

STEP 3: After the children have jumped, collect the jump ropes and have the jumpers be seated.

SAY: How many jumps were counted. Wow! You all counted [number of jumps]! We have a lot of joyful hearts here, don't we? One of the ways to be joyful is to think of all things that make us happy. These are ways our lives have been blessed by God. When we count our blessings it fills our heart with joy. Next time you are sad, count your blessings and God will help you feel joyful.

DISCUSSION QUESTIONS

1. How do you think a cheerful (or joyful) heart affects us?

2. Where do you think our inner joy comes from?

3. How is the joy God gives us different from other kinds of joy?

LIFE APPLICATION

SAY: True joy doesn't come from things. It comes from God. The joy God gives us can't be taken away no matter what is happening around us.

Wrap It Up

SAY: Our friends who jumped earlier jumped [number of times] because their hearts were filled with joy. True joy comes from God and fills us with so much excitement that we can't help but jump with excitement!

Chapter 58: Strong Foundation

Scripture: "No one can lay any other foundation than what has already been laid. That foundation is Jesus Christ." – 1 Corinthians 3:11

Topic
Strong foundation

Purpose

To illustrate that a strong foundation in Christ gives what we build the best chance of standing.

Type:

Games
Action

Supplies:

- Building bricks (20 for each group of 4-5 children)
- Sandwich sized plastic bags (1 bag per 4-5 children)

Preparation

Place 20 building bricks in each bag. Use a variety of sizes in each bag.

PRESENTATION

SAY: When someone is asked to build something, they have a lot of important steps to take care of before building starts. For example, they have to make sure they have all of the right building supplies. They might also find it helpful to have a blueprint that gives them instructions on how to build. They would also need workers to do the building. Today, you're going to work together to build something using the materials and instructions I give you.

STEP 1: Divide the children into groups of 4-5.

STEP 2: Give each group a bag of building bricks.

SAY: We are going to try an experiment. This group *(point to one group)* needs to build using bricks from the largest on top to smallest on the bottom. This group *(point to the other group)* needs to build a structure using bricks from smallest on top to the largest on the bottom.

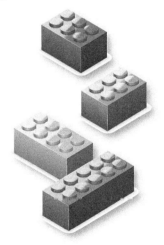

Take It Further

Connect this object lesson to other Bible passages:
- The Wise and Foolish Builders (Matthew 7:24-27)
- Firm Foundation (Isaiah 28:16)
- Most Important Stone (Psalm 118:22)

STEP 3: Give time for them to complete it.

SAY: Was it more challenging to build with the largest on top and smallest on the bottom or smallest on top and largest on the bottom? Putting the larger blocks on the bottom gave us a stronger foundation. The Bible talks about a foundation in our life.

STEP 4: Read 1 Corinthians 3:11.

SAY: When the foundation of our lives is Jesus, we can withstand whatever may come and try to knock us down. We can make Jesus our foundation when we give him control of our life. We ask him to forgive us and become Christians, then we stay close to him by reading the Bible and praying.

DISCUSSION QUESTIONS

1. Which structure was the most steady?
2. Why was having the largest bricks on the bottom better?
3. Is Jesus in your life helping you stand strong?

LIFE APPLICATION

SAY: When we are building something that we want to last, it's important to have the best possible foundation.

Wrap It Up

SAY: We can build a strong foundation by trusting Jesus as our Savior and growing our relationship with him by attending church regularly, reading our Bibles, praying, and listening to him. Are you ready to build a strong foundation?

Chapter 59: Heart of the Matter

Scripture: "In the same way, the Spirit helps us in our weakness. We do not know what we ought to pray for, but the Spirit himself intercedes for us through wordless groans."
– Romans 8:26, NIV

Topic
Prayer

Purpose
To illustrate that our words don't have to be perfect when we pray because God looks at our heart.

Type:
Games

Supplies:
- Letter tiles
- Small brown paper lunch bag
- Table or other hard surface

Preparation
Gather letter tiles that spell the following words:
- "ASK",
- "THANK"
- "TRUST"

PRESENTATION

SAY: I love word games, especially games when I have to make words out of letter tiles.

STEP 1: Hold up the letter tiles for the children to see.

SAY: Sometimes I get just the right letters but other times I don't have the right letters to build the words I want. Have you ever felt like you just didn't have the right words? *(Allow answers).*

Have you ever felt that way when you pray? *(Allow answers).* There are so many needs that people around us have and so much happening in our world that sometimes, we just don't know what to pray. It can feel like our words are all mixed up.

STEP 2: Place the letter tiles in the brown paper bag and shake it up.

SAY: You might even feel afraid to pray because you're not sure your words will come out of your mouth the right way.

Take It Further
Connect this object lesson to other Bible passages:
- Moses Feels Inadequate (Exodus 4:1-17)
- God Looks at the Heart (1 Samuel 16:7)
- God is Ready (Psalm 118:22)

Object Lesson: Prayer

When we pray, we don't have to worry about how our words sound because God looks at our heart.

STEP 3: Read Romans 8:26.

SAY: Wow, the Holy Spirit helps us pray. Let's see how.

STEP 4: Spell out **ASK.**

SAY: When we don't know what to pray we can **ASK** God to help us.

STEP 5: Spell out **THANKS.**

SAY: When we don't know what to pray, we can **THANK** God for what he's done and what he's going to do. Thank him that he knows our hearts and doesn't need perfect words.

STEP 6: Spell out **TRUST.**

SAY: When we don't know what to pray, we can **TRUST** God to work it all out. We can be so grateful that we don't have to pray perfectly. He hears us and knows what we mean and what we need.

DISCUSSION QUESTIONS

1. What types of things do you pray for?

2. Do you find it easy or hard to pray?

3. What can you do in those times when you don't know what to pray?

LIFE APPLICATION

SAY: Our words don't have to be perfect when we pray because God looks at our heart. He is more concerned with our attitude than our words.

Wrap It Up

SAY: Remember, God looks at our heart, not our words, when we pray. He hears us regardless.

Chapter 60: Oops – Sorry!

Scripture: "But God is faithful and fair. If we admit that we have sinned, he will forgive us our sins. He will forgive every wrong thing we have done. He will make us pure."
– 1 John 1:9

Topic Apologizing

Purpose

To help children understand the importance of saying "I'm sorry".

Type:
Games

Supplies:
- Board game

Preparation

Set up the board game as if you were ready to play.

PRESENTATION

SAY: Playing board games with a friend can be awesome! This is one of my favorite board games to play.

STEP 1: Hold up the game board.

SAY: You can see on this board that there is a place you start and the object is to get home. Many things happen to you along the way. You draw cards that tell you what to do. Sometimes you get ahead and sometimes you fall behind. The goal is to get home, to the safe zone.

STEP 2: Show the pieces.

SAY: Let's pretend the players are you and me and all the people around us. The board is our life. Home is living for all eternity with God in heaven. That is where we all want to end up. As we travel through life sometimes we do wrong

Take It Further

Connect this object lesson to other Bible passages:
- Live in Peace (Romans 12:18)
- Confess to One Another (James 5:16)
- God Forgives (Hebrews 8:12)

things and sometimes others do wrong things to us. In the game if you land on a square with another player in it they have to go all the way back to start. *(Model this with the pieces.)* This may be when we have done something wrong to someone and hurt them. When this happens we need to be willing to say we are sorry and make it right if we can.

STEP 3: Model a piece knocking you back to start.

SAY: Sometimes someone does something to hurt you. It is important to forgive them when they apologize. Saying "I'm sorry" in a game is easy and a little fun but saying "I'm sorry" in real life is a bit harder. The Bible tells us that all of us have sinned, or done things that were wrong. God models forgiveness to us.

STEP 4: Read 1 John 1:19.

SAY: God forgives us when we ask for forgiveness. He wants us to forgive others. Being able to see when you are wrong and say sorry is very important.

DISCUSSION QUESTIONS

1. Have you ever had to say "I'm sorry" for hurting someone?

2. What was the outcome?

3. How can you show forgiveness when someone has wronged you?

LIFE APPLICATION

SAY: When we hurt someone, either on purpose or by accident, it is important to say "I'm sorry" to restore the relationship. God wants us to live at peace with everyone.

Wrap It Up

SAY: Saying "I'm sorry" and asking for forgiveness isn't easy but it's necessary for relationships to be in the right place. It takes courage to admit when we're wrong but it also shows our character.

Chapter 61: Jesus, the Best Gift

Scripture: "God did not send his Son into the world to judge the world. He sent his Son to save the world through him." – John 3:17

Topic
Love of God

Purpose
To illustrate that the best gift is God's love for you by sending Jesus.

Type:
Everyday objects

Supplies:

- 2 Christmas wrapped gift boxes or bags
- Tissue paper
- A picture/figurine of Jesus in the manger
- Small candy bar

Preparation

Place the picture of Jesus in the manger in one bag. Place the candy bar inside the other bag. **If using the gift bags, insert tissue paper after the envelopes are placed inside.
Set the bags on a table or on the floor in front of your presentation area.

PRESENTATION

SAY: How many of you love to celebrate Christmas? *(Allow answers).* Christmas is such a special time of year! One nice part of Christmas is when people who love us give us gifts. Usually, your loved ones have thought about what you like, need, or will make you happy before picking the perfect gift.

STEP 1: Show the two bags.

SAY: I have a few gifts here. In one is a gift that someone, who loves you very much, picked out just for you. In the other is an okay gift. Which one do you think has the best gift? *(Allow answers)*

STEP 2: Open up the bag with the candy.

SAY: I wonder what is in this bag. *(Rustle around and pull out the candy bar.)* Mmm, candy. We like getting candy. If I eat this candy right now, what will I have when it is gone? *(Allow answers)* That's right, nothing.

Take It Further

Connect this object lesson to other Bible passages:
- Jesus is Born (Luke 2)
- Prophecy of Jesus' Birth (Isaiah 9:6-7)
- God Sent Jesus (Galatians 4:4)

Object Lesson: Love of God

STEP 3: Open the next bag.

SAY: The gift in this bag was picked especially for you. A lot of love went into picking it out. The one who picked it out knows everything about you. What you like and don't like, what you love, and need. Let's look. *(Pull out the picture or figurine of Jesus as a baby)* What is this? It represents the gift of Jesus coming as a baby. He was born a man, but was still God. God sent him to grow up and die on the cross for your sins. What an amazing present. Because of Jesus we can forever be with God! Just like all gifts, we cannot have the gift unless we take it and open it. We have to accept the gift of salvation through Christ. How long will this gift last? *(Allow answers)* That's right, forever.

STEP 4: Read John 3:17.

SAY: This verse tells us the reason why God sent his Son, Jesus, into the world: to save the world through him. We cannot be saved without a Savior. Best gift ever!

DISCUSSION QUESTIONS

1. What do you love most about Christmas?

2. Does your family celebrate Jesus at Christmastime? How?

3. Would you celebrate Christmas differently if Jesus wasn't a part of it?

LIFE APPLICATION

SAY: God's greatest gift to us at Christmas couldn't be bought in a store. It was given to us in a manger. His name was Jesus.

Wrap It Up

SAY: We need to remember to focus on Jesus at Christmastime. Thank God for bringing you the best gift ever, Jesus!

Chapter 62: Make Room for Jesus

Scripture: "She gave birth to her first baby. It was a boy. She wrapped him in large strips of cloth. Then she placed him in a manger. There was no room in for them in the inn." – Luke 2:7

Topic
Remember Jesus

Purpose
To help children not forget the real meaning of Christmas.

Type:
Everyday objects
Messy

Supplies:
- Decorated Christmas tree
- Wrapped boxes and gift bags (enough to cover the entire base of the tree)
- Roll or two of wrapping paper

Preparation

Plan to make this presentation near the decorated Christmas tree.

PRESENTATION

STEP 1: Enter the presentation area carrying the roll of wrapping paper. *(For added fun, have tape stuck to your face and wrapping paper twirled around you. Mess up your hair.)*

SAY: Oh my goodness, I have been so busy wrapping presents. I mean look at all of these presents! And I still have so many more to wrap. When I look at all of the presents that are under my tree *(point to the gifts under your tree)* and think about all of the gifts I haven't wrapped yet, I think I might run out of room. Did you know that on the night Jesus was born, there was no room for him?

STEP 2: Read Luke 2:7.

SAY: Usually when babies are born, there are two rooms ready for them: one at the

Take It Further

Connect this object lesson to other Bible passages:
- Jesus, Born to Save (Matthew 1:21)
- Be Still (Psalm 46:10)
- Word Became Flesh (John 1:14)

hospital where they will be born and one in their house. When Jesus was born, there was no hospital room for him, just a manger in a stable. At Christmastime, we can forget to focus on Jesus. With all that happens that we get distracted with, we need to make sure that we spend time focusing on Jesus.

DISCUSSION QUESTIONS

1. How do you get ready to celebrate Christmas?
2. Have you ever taken the time to read the Christmas story from the Bible?
3. What do you think about there being no room for baby Jesus when he was born?

LIFE APPLICATION

SAY: Years and years ago, Jesus was born in a stable. Today, as we rush to get everything ready to celebrate Christmas, we might make no room for Jesus. We can forget all about why we celebrate Christmas. Let's not forget the real reason we celebrate – Jesus was born for us.

Wrap It Up

SAY: As we go about decorating, shopping, baking, and visiting family and friends, let's be sure to make room for Jesus in all of that. After all, if it wasn't for him, we wouldn't celebrate Christmas!

Chapter 63: Easter -Jump the Gap

Scripture: For the wages (payment) of sin is death, but the gift of God is eternal life in Christ Jesus our Lord.   – Romans 6:23

Topic
Our Sin

Type:
Kid Volunteer, Everyday objects

Supplies:
- 2 mats
- 3 pieces of paper/ marker
- Tape

Preparation
- Write 'God', 'Us', and 'Jesus' each on their own piece of paper.
- Tape the 'God' sign to one mat and the 'Us' sign to the other mat. Hold on to the Jesus sign for later in the lesson.
- Place rolled up tape under the mats to help them not slip when jumped on.

Purpose
To help children recognize their sin and need for Jesus.

PRESENTATION

SAY: This time of year we have a holiday we celebrate called Easter. We know that Jesus died on the cross and rose from the dead on the third day. How many of you can tell me why? *(Show of hands)* Wow that is great! Many of you know why. I am going to talk to you today about why Jesus had to die on the cross.

STEP 1: Hold up the two mats.

> **SAY:** I have a mat that represents God and a mat that represents us.

STEP 2: Place the two mats close to each other. Ask a few kids to jump from one mat to the other.

> **SAY:** You were able to cross over from one mat to the other really easy. Can someone tell me an   example of something one of you could do that is wrong? *(Allow answers)*

STEP 3: After each child shares an example, move the "God" mat and have a child jump from one to the other until they can no longer make it.

Take It Further

Connect this object lesson to other Bible passages:
- Children of God (John 1:12)
- Gave his son (John 3:16)
- Confess our sins (Romans 10:9)

Object Lesson: Our Sin

SAY: When we do wrong things, or sin, it causes us to be so separated from God that we can't be with him. This made God sad. God wanted to be close to us.

STEP 4: Read 1 Peter 3:18

SAY: This verse says the payment for sin is death. *(In this case death mean forever separated from God for all eternity.)* God sent Jesus to die in our place, to pay the penalty for our sin so that we would be able to be with God for all eternity instead of separated. So when Jesus died the gap between us and God was moved. *(Move the God mat back over, and place the Jesus sign between 'Us' and 'God' mats. Close enough to jump to)* This is GREAT! We can be with God now. However, one thing is different. In order for you to be with God you have to accept Jesus as your Savior. *(Allow a child to stand on the 'Us' mat, pick up the Jesus sign and step over to the God mat.)*

STEP 5: Depending on your group, you can go into a salvation message or conclude the lesson.

DISCUSSION QUESTIONS

1. Have you sinned?

2. What would happen if you accepted Jesus as your Savior?

3. Can you have a relationship with God forever?

LIFE APPLICATION

SAY: We have done wrong things in our life, but God sent a way to be forgiven.

Wrap It Up

SAY: When you sin or do wrong things, you are separating yourself from God. We ask God for forgiveness and invite Jesus to be in charge of our life. Then we can be with God forever. We have to choose.

Chapter 64: A Love Like No Other

Scripture: "But here is how God has shown his love for us. While we were still sinners, Christ died for us." – Romans 5:8

Topic
Forgiven

Purpose
To help children reflect on God's great, sacrificial love for them.

Type:
Everyday objects
Action

Supplies:
- Wooden/paper cross (any size, but the bigger the better)
- Sticky notes
- Pens/markers

Preparation
Set the wooden or paper cross at the front or center of your presentation area.

PRESENTATION

SAY: How do you know someone loves you? *(Allow answers)* We all feel love in different ways - some of us like to hear kind words such as, "I'm so proud of you" or "I love you". Some like to receive gifts or a helping hand. Others like all of those things!

When I reflect on Jesus's love, I can't help but notice that he showed love for all of humanity by his words and his actions. He said, "I love you" and then showed that by giving his life so that we could have eternal life. The way he showed the ultimate measure of love was so selfless and undeserved.

STEP 1: Stand by the wooden cross and read Romans 5:8. .

> **SAY:** When we look at a cross, we can be reminded of God's great love for us. He loved us so much that he gave his one and only Son for us. We will never, ever know of a more sacrificial love than that.

STEP 2: Give each child a sticky note and marker/pen.

Take It Further
Connect this object lesson to other Bible passages:
- No More Death (Revelation 21:4)
- Saved By Grace (Ephesians 2:8-9)
- Jesus, Our Promise Keeper (2 Peter 3:9)

Object Lesson:
Forgiven

SAY: I want everyone to take this and turn it over to the sticky side. On this side take a moment to write something you have done wrong and need forgiveness for on your sticky note. No one will read it or see it. This is just between you and God. *(Allow time for this)* I see most of you are done. Take a moment to pray over your paper. Ask God to forgive you for what you did. *(Allow time for this.)* Turn it over and draw a heart on the front.

STEP 3: Invite the children to bring their sticky notes up and place them on the cross.

SAY: Jesus made it possible for us to be forgiven for our sins. No one will ever love you more than Jesus. We need to always accept his gift of love and sacrifice.

STEP 4: Depending on your group, you can go into a salvation message or conclude the lesson.

DISCUSSION QUESTIONS

1. Do you think you deserve God's love?
2. Is there anything you can do for God not to love you?
3. How can you show Jesus how grateful you are that he loves you?

LIFE APPLICATION

SAY: I believe that all of us want to feel loved. The love that Jesus showed for us when he died for us was the greatest act of love. He sacrificed his life so that we can live with him forever.

Wrap It Up

SAY: God loved us before the beginning of time and had a plan, even then, to send his son to prove to us how much. It wasn't something we deserved but received through grace. Have you received the gracious gift of love Jesus has to offer?

Chapter 65: Honor Your Father

Scripture: *"A wise son brings joy to his father."*
– Proverbs 10:1, NIV

Topic
Honor Dad

Purpose
To help children understand a few ways to honor their dads.

Type:
Everyday objects

Supplies:
- Eraser
- Bible
- Some type of tool (like a hammer, a wrench, or a screwdriver)

Preparation
None

PRESENTATION

SAY: Today is Father's Day! It's a day that we celebrate dads, grandpas, uncles, and other men who are like fathers to us. We honor them for all of the ways they love us and take care of us.

STEP 1: Read Proverbs 10:1.

SAY: There are a few ways that I think sons (and daughters) can honor their dads or make them happy. Some of you may not have dads in your life right now. This can apply to anyone in your life God has given you to help you grow into a great person.

STEP 2: Hold up the eraser.

SAY: Erasers help us to get rid of the things we've done wrong so that we can make things right. The Bible tells us that children are disciplined by their father. No one likes to be disciplined but a father's good, healthy discipline helps us to learn from our mistakes so that we stay out of trouble. We can honor this important person by learning from our mistakes and listening to his wisdom.

Take It Further
Connect this object lesson to other Bible passages:
- Honor Your Father & Mother (Ephesians 6:2)
- Hearts in Tune (Malachi 4:6)
- Get Your Father's Wisdom (Proverbs 4:1)

Object Lesson:
Honor Dad

STEP 3: Hold up the Bible.

> **SAY:** When our important adult loves Jesus, it helps us learn to love Jesus too. They might bring us to church, pray with us and for us, and read the Bible to us and with us. If we are wise, we will listen to this person talk about Jesus so that we can grow to love Jesus too.

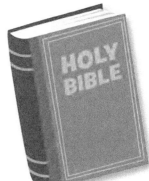

STEP 4: Hold up the tool.

> **SAY:** Many times this person can fix things around the house or bring in someone to fix it. If we are wise, we'll watch them and possibly learn how to fix things too. This person care of their family because they love them and want them to live in a safe place. God brings these important people into our life to teach us. We need to do our part and learn from them.

? DISCUSSION QUESTIONS

1. What important people are you celebrating today?
2. What things do they teach you?
3. How can you show them honor today and every day?

LIFE APPLICATION

SAY: These special people are such a blessing to us. God gave them to us to help us learn how to love, nurture, and protect our families. They are great gifts to our families and we should honor them today and every day.

Wrap It Up

SAY: If we take the time to listen to these important people, we can learn so much that will help us now and down the road when we're grown-ups.

Chapter 66: Sunday's Coming

Scripture: "...weeping may stay for the night, but rejoicing comes in the morning." – Psalm 30:5, NIV

Topic
A Way Across

Purpose
To give children hope that although the death of Jesus is sad, joy is right around the corner.

Type:
Kid Volunteer,
Everyday Objects

Supplies:
- Three boards
- Tissues
  (one per child)
- Markers

Preparation
- Set 2 boards on the ground parallel to each other too far apart for someone to jump from one to the other.
- Set the third board aside for later in the lesson.

Optional:
Label each board:
God, Us, Jesus

PRESENTATION

SAY: On Good Friday, we remember the death and burial of our Savior, Jesus. It's a day that many feel is anything but good. Why is it called Good? Who can name some good things? *(Allow answers)* Those are good things. But sometimes things that don't seem good lead to a good thing. Having to take medicine, getting in trouble for something you did wrong that could hurt you, and things like that. We were separated from God because of sin.

STEP 1: Point to one board as God and one board as us.

SAY: There was no way to get to God. (**Optional:** have a child try and jump from one board to the other.) Jesus died on the cross so we could cross over this huge gap and get to God. Jesus had to die for us. The Bible says the wages of sin is death. We deserved to die for our sin, not go to heaven. None of us are worthy of that. But God loved us so much that he sent Jesus to take our place and die for our sins, even though he had never sinned. That he had to die for us is sad!

Take It Further

Connect this object lesson to other Bible passages:
- Death Doesn't Win (1 Corinthians 15:55)
- Mourning into Dancing (Psalm 30:11)
- Grief into Joy (John 16:20)

 Top 50 Object Lessons: Games & Activities

STEP 2: Place the third board across the other two to connect them and create a bridge.

SAY: Even though on Good Friday Jesus died and that is so very sad, it created the ability for us to cross over and be with God now. That is GOOD! So even though a super sad thing happened on this day, it is the best GOOD ever! It makes it possible for us to be with GOD! *(Allow a volunteer kid to cross the board.)*

STEP 3: Distribute one tissue to each child. Read Psalm 30:5.

SAY: This verse tells us that even though the events of this day are so sad, our joy comes when we know that on Easter morning Jesus rose from the dead and is alive today! We use tissues when we cry and are sad. Take a marker and draw a happy face on it. Take these home to remember that even when we are sad about what Jesus had to do for us, we can be happy we can have a relationship with God now.

DISCUSSION QUESTIONS

1. What are some things that come to mind about Jesus dying on the cross?
2. How does that make you feel?
3. How does knowing Sunday's coming impact your thinking?

LIFE APPLICATION

SAY: Death is not a happy time, but although the death of Jesus is sad, we can have joy because Sunday's coming! He defeated death and rose again. He lives in heaven today and that is good news!

Wrap It Up

SAY: It is sometimes confusing to call this day good. Take your tissue home and tell someone that the good news comes on Sunday. Invite them to church with you.

Chapter 67: Crown Jewel

Scripture: "Gray hair is a glorious crown. You get it by living the right way." – Proverbs 16:31, NIRV

Topic
Give Honor

Purpose
To celebrate the wisdom our grandparents have.

Type:
Everyday objects

Supplies:
- Gray wig

Preparation
Put the wig on before entering your presentation area.

Optional:
Show a picture of someone with gray hair if you can't locate a wig.

PRESENTATION

SAY: Today is a GRAND DAY to celebrate who's GRAND in our lives. It's Grandparent's Day! I think grandparents are pretty cool people. Most grandparents have lived a long time and have seen a lot of things. Along the way, they have picked up a lot of wisdom. My hair is gray. Does that mean I am wise? *(Point to the wig and toss your head.)* Well no, of course this is a wig. When you see a person with gray hair, you might think they're old. They might be. But what if we looked at gray hair a little differently.

STEP 1: Read Proverbs 16:31.

SAY: This verse tells us two important things:

1. Gray hair is a glorious crown. Who usually wears a crown? *(Allow answers.)* Yes, kings, queens, and other royal people usually wear crowns. This tells us we need to honor our grandparents. How do you do that? *(Allow answers).* You need to treat them with respect even if what they say or do seems different from how you would do it.

2. You get gray hair by living a longer time. They have lived longer than us or our parents and so they have learned a lot

Take It Further

Connect this object lesson to other Bible passages:
- Passed-down Stories (Joel 1:3)
- Keeping the Past Alive (Deuteronomy 4:9)
- House Built By Wisdom (Proverbs 24:3)

 Top 50 Object Lessons: Games & Activities

over the years. They can take what they've learned and pass it on to us. How can you learn what your grandparents know? *(Allow answers)* That's right. Let them tell you stories, ask them questions, spend time talking with them.

DISCUSSION QUESTIONS

1. If we think of grandparents as royalty instead of just grandparents, how might we treat them different.

2. What is one thing you've learned from your grandparents?

3. How can you show honor to your grandparents today?

LIFE APPLICATION

SAY: Like our parents, our grandparents love us and want only the best for us. They have a lot of wisdom about life to share with us and if we're wise, we'll listen.

Wrap It Up

SAY: If your grandparents have a lot of gray hair, don't just see them as old. See them as wise. All of their gray hair means they've lived the right way, so listen to them.

Chapter 68: Battle Fight

Scripture: "The Lord will fight for you.
Just be still." – Exodus 14:14

Topic
God's Help

Purpose
To help children understand that that we cannot fight our battles without God's help.

Type:
Kid Volunteer

Supplies:
- Tug of war rope
- Painter's tape
- Chair

Preparation
Use the painter's tape to mark a center line in the tug of war playing area. Tape off where each side will start. Don't make it too far apart. You need room for a chair in the middle and maybe 4 feet on each side.

PRESENTATION

SAY: When someone is fighting for their independence, that means that something or someone is holding them captive. They cannot move on their own and are at the command of someone else. On July 4, the United States of America celebrates its Independence as its own country. By being free, we are now able to make our own rules and set up the type of government we want. There is another way to be captive. In our life we have to struggle with the choices we make. Sometimes it is hard to do the right thing. It can feel like we are captive and can't move away from the wrong thing. But is that really true?

STEP 1: Show the rope.

SAY: Let's pretend this rope is our life, and the choices we make and who we are becoming. I need a volunteer. You, *(Point to the volunteer)* are the person this life *(point to the rope)* represents. I am going to represent bad choices. Now who wants us

Take It Further
Connect this object lesson to other Bible passages:
- Flesh vs. Blood (Ephesians 6:12)
- Apostle Paul Shares Good News in Prison (Philippians 1:12-26)
- Joseph and Potiphar's Wife (Genesis 39)

to make bad choices? *(Allow answers)* That's right, Satan wants to trip us up and have us do the wrong thing. He is on the other end trying to pull us toward bad choices. Now everyone needs to be cheering for *(name the child)*.

STEP 2: Each of you take an end of the rope. Place the taped line at the top of the chair so you will know who is winning. Tell the child to pull on the rope and try to win. Have the class cheer on the child pulling against the bad choices. (You) After a minute let the child win. Thank him/her and have them take a seat.

SAY: Well he/she really needed to work hard to win and make good choices. How do we win at making good choices in real life? *(Allow answers).* That's right. We need to stay close to God, pray, read our Bible, surround ourselves with good people, and go to church. God will help us win our independence over bad choices and make good ones.

STEP 3: Read Exodus 14:14.

SAY: We may have to work hard to make good choices, but God is in the battle with us. He is helping us when we ask him to help us.

DISCUSSION QUESTIONS

1. Is there a battle you're facing right now that seems too tough for you?

2. Have you prayed and asked God for help?

3. What might it look like for you to not fight this battle but let God instead?

LIFE APPLICATION

SAY: Some of you might be facing a tough challenge right now that might seem impossible to win. Be encouraged - God is with you in this fight! He wants you to win and with his help, you will!

Wrap It Up

SAY: God doesn't want us to fight battles on our own. He wants to be right there, fighting for us.

Top 50 Object Lessons: Games & Activities

Chapter 69: Mom's Purse

Scripture: "My son, listen to your father's advice. Don't turn away from your mother's teaching."
– Proverbs 1:8-33

**Topic
Ready**

Purpose
To help children recognize all their moms do.

Type:
Everyday objects

Supplies:
- Purse
- Packaged snack
- Tissues
- Medicine bottle
- Duster or sponge
- Dish soap
- Comb/brush
- Small Bible

Preparation
Make sure everything is in the purse

Tip
Be sensitive to anyone in your class that does not have their mom in their life. Change your language about mom to say, mom or another special person God has given you to care for you.

PRESENTATION

STEP 1: Pull out a big purse.

SAY: What is this? *(Allow answers)* That's right, it's a purse. Does your mom carry a purse? *(Allow answers)* Isn't it amazing how many things come out of your mom's purse? It seems like every time I needed something it was in my mom's purse. Let's have a look

STEP 2: Pull out a snack.

SAY: Yes, a snack. No matter what, my mom always made sure I ate all my meals. Even when I got hungry in between, mom had a snack ready to go. She always made sure I ate healthy so I would grow strong and develop good eating habits. How about your mom?

STEP 3: Pull out the comb/brush.

SAY: My mom always made sure I had clothes to wear and taught me how to get myself ready each day. How about your mom? Do

Take It Further
Connect this object lesson to other Bible passages:
- Hannah and Samuel (1 Samuel 1)
- Ruth and Naomi (Ruth 1)
- Mary, the Mother of Jesus (Luke 2:19)

you have to worry about having clothes each morning?

STEP 4: Pull out the tissues and medicine bottle.

SAY: Ah yes, my mom was the best when I was sick or sad. She would give me hugs and kisses, bring me soup and medicine. Or when I was sad give me comfort. Moms are so nice when we need special attention.

STEP 5: Pull out the duster and dish soap.

SAY: Can you imagine what our houses would look like if mom and dad never cleaned anything! They clean the dishes, the laundry, and pick up messes. They even make sure we are clean. Without them we would be a mess and everything around us would be a mess.

STEP 6: Pull out the Bible.

SAY: The Bible talks about moms. Let me read. *(Read Proverbs 1:8.)* Don't turn away from your mother's teaching. We need to listen to our mothers. See all the things she does. Tell her we love her, listen to all she says, and really appreciate her for all she does.

DISCUSSION QUESTIONS

1. Why is listening to your mom important?
2. Why do you think it's important to God?
3. What are some ways that you can show your mom you love her?

LIFE APPLICATION

SAY: Moms are very special people and deserve to be celebrated on their special day – and every day.

Wrap It Up

SAY: Watch all the things your mom does this week. As you see her doing something for you, the family, or the house, thank her and help her. Listen to all she has to teach you.

Chapter 70: Lifetime Teacher

Scripture: "Honor your father and mother." That is the first commandment that has a promise." "Then things will go well with you. You will live a long time on the earth."
– Ephesians 6:2-3

Topic
Life Lessons

Purpose
To help children understand that what a mom teaches stays with us for a lifetime.

Type:
Action

Supplies:
- 2 pieces of poster board
- Black marker

Preparation
Use the marker to write the words "Do's" on one poster board and "Don'ts" on the other poster board.

Tip
Be sensitive to anyone in your class that does not have their mom in their life. Change your language about mom to say, mom or another special person God has given you to care for you.

PRESENTATION

SAY: Today we're celebrating our moms! We are celebrating them because of all of the love they give us, all of the things they do for us and for all of things they've taught us. Whether we're young or old, we can still learn a thing or two from our moms. I bet you all have learned a lot from your mom already even though you're not as old as me. Let me see what all you've learned.

STEP 1: Hold up the posters.

> **SAY:** I have two posters here. What do they say? *(Allow answers)* That's right, Do's and Don'ts. We are going to have fun for a minute and have a contest.

STEP 2: Divide the group into 2 groups. Give one group the "Do's" poster and one group the "Don'ts" poster.

> **SAY:** This group *(point to the Do's group)* is going to come up with as many things as they can remember that their mom says to do. For instance, "Do your homework, take out the trash, etc.) This group *(Point to the Don't group)* is

Take It Further

Connect this object lesson to other Bible passages:
- A Wise Man Listens (Proverbs 12:15)
- Listen and Accept Correction (Proverbs 19:20)
- Guard Instruction (Proverbs 4:13)

going to think of all the things moms tell us not to do like, don't pick your nose, don't eat cookies before dinner, etc. Let's see which group can come up with the most. Go! *(Allow time for this)*

STEP 3: Draw their attention back to you. Have them bring up the posters.

SAY: Wow, our moms spend a lot of time directing us. Why do you think they do that? Wouldn't they rather just relax and read a book, or do something more fun? *(Allow answers)* Moms do this because they love us. They want us to grow strong, be safe and good people. Sometimes we can have an attitude about all the Do's and Don'ts we are told. Let's see what the Bible says.

STEP 4: Read Ephesians 6:2-3.

SAY: When we listen and treat our parents with respect, God promises it will go well for us. God uses our mom and dad to help our life go better. When we fight against this our life does not go well. We have problems, fights, we get sick, or are not safe. Honoring means to listen and treat them well. The next time your mom tells you to do or don't do something, know it is out of love.

DISCUSSION QUESTIONS

1. Does it seem like your mom has a long list of rules?

2. Do you follow those rules or do you question and disobey them?

3. How can you better listen to the teaching your mom is giving you?

LIFE APPLICATION

SAY: God gave us moms so that we can grow up to be caring, loving people. It may seem like she only gives us lists of do's and don'ts, but what a mom teaches stays with us a lifetime.

Wrap It Up

SAY: Today and every day, treasure what your mom is trying to teach you. Trust her words because she loves you and wants the best for you.

Chapter 71: **Pass the Praise**

Scripture: *"Always give thanks to God the Father for everything. Give thanks to him in the name of our Lord Jesus Christ."* – Ephesians 5:20

Topic
Praise God

Purpose
To illustrate how Thanksgiving is more than a meal –it's a time to offer praise to God for our blessings.

Type:
Everyday objects
Action

Supplies:
- Cornucopia or picture of one
- Slips of paper
- Markers

Alternate Idea:
If you don't have a cornucopia, use a picture to explain it then use a basket to collect the praise papers in.

Preparation
Set all of the supplies in an easily-accessible part of your presentation area.

PRESENTATION

SAY: This week, families all across America will gather with family and friends to celebrate Thanksgiving. I love Thanksgiving because it's just that...a day to give thanks. On days like Thanksgiving, it can be easy to give thanks. We plan to spend time with family and friends, eat a delicious meal, watch a little football and relax. Life is good and well, we're thankful. Sometimes it's hard, though, to give thanks because things aren't always going well. People get sick. Friends move away. People don't get along. It can be hard to be thankful in circumstances like that. It can be difficult to find reasons to be thankful when things aren't going too great. The Bible tells us that being thankful isn't optional. It doesn't matter if things are going well or not. We are instructed to always give thanks.

STEP 1: Read Ephesians 5:20.

SAY: God reminds us to give thanks to him. This isn't so he can hear all the great things he has done and given you. It is for us. When we focus on what to be thankful for it fills our heart and mind with the right focus. If we focus in on what is wrong, we are sad and miserable all the time. God wants us to

Take It Further
Connect this object lesson to other Bible passages:
- Give Thanks to the Lord (Psalm 107:1)
- Proclaim the Lord (1 Chronicles 16:8)
- Grateful Praise (Psalm 100:1-5)

 Top 50 Object Lessons: Games & Activities

Object Lesson: Praise God

recognize the good we have so we can live a life that brings him honor and fills our days we thankfulness instead of sadness and anger.

STEP 2: Hold up the cornucopia or the picture.

SAY: Does anyone know what this is? What is it used for? *(Allow answers)* Yes, this cornucopia *(or horn of plenty)* is traditionally used at Thanksgiving as a symbol of abundance. It can be filled with fruits, vegetables, flowers, or nuts. Today we're going to fill our cornucopia *(or horn of plenty)* with praises to God. Let's try to fill it to overflowing!

STEP 3: Hand out pieces of paper and pencils.

SAY: Take a slip or two of paper and write something you would like to praise God for. Then fold the paper in half and place it inside the cornucopia. *(Allow time for this.)* We have filled this horn of plenty with plenty of praise. Let's read a few. *(Adjust this according to your time.)* We have so much to be thankful for. We need to always remember to thank God all the time for what he has given us and done for us.

DISCUSSION QUESTIONS

1. Was it easy or difficult to find something to praise God for?
2. Have you ever felt like you have nothing to be thankful for?
3. What have you done in those times?

LIFE APPLICATION

SAY: A thankful heart isn't just thankful on a holiday focused on giving thanks. A thankful heart always has a reason to praise.

Wrap It Up

SAY: God doesn't want our praises and thanksgivings to be limited to just one day. He wants us to have a lifestyle of thanksgiving by praising him everyday, in all things. Having a lifestyle of thanksgiving means trusting God with the good and the bad and thanking him regardless.

Chapter 72: Thank You

Scripture: "I thank my God every time I remember you." – Philippians 1:3, NIV

Topic Appreciate

Purpose
To help children to say thank you to someone they appreciate.

Type:
Food

Supplies:
- Ear of corn or can of corn
- Thank-you card (Especially one that is special to you.)

Preparation

None

PRESENTATION

SAY: This time of year we celebrate Thanksgiving. The pilgrims wanted to pause and recognize the provision that God had given them to survive in this new land. We take time each year to gather with family and friends and be grateful and thankful for what God has done for us. God gives us a place to live, food, and loved ones to be in our life. We have a church and friends that bring so much to our life.

STEP 1: Read Philippians 1:3.

> **SAY:** God tells us in the Bible that we should pause and thank God for people in our life he has given us.

STEP 2: Hold an ear of corn. (Or can of corn if you can't get an ear.)

> **SAY:** Who knows what this is? *(Allow answers)* That is right, it is corn. Corn was a big part of the first Thanksgiving. The settlers were taught about corn, or maze, by the Indians. They invited the Indians to Thanksgiving to thank them for their

Take It Further

Connect this object lesson to other Bible passages:
- Hannah Says Thanks (1 Samuel 2)
- Mary Says Thanks (Luke 1:46-55)
- The Healed Leper Says Thanks (Luke 17:11-19)

 Top 50 Object Lessons: Games & Activities

help. We have people in our life that help us. We need to remember to thank them for all they do for us.

STEP 3: Hold up a thank-you card.

SAY: I have a thank-you card here that is special to me. *(Tell why)* When someone goes out of their way to say thank you to you it is very special. You know they are thinking of you and appreciate you. There are people in our life we should tell thank you to. Who can name some people that we should say thank you to? *(Allow answers)* Wow, God has given us so many people to be grateful for. When we see them or remember them we need to thank them for the special things they do just like in our verse.

DISCUSSION QUESTIONS

1. Is it easy or difficult for you to say 'thank you'?

2. What stops you from saying 'thanks' more?

3. Who is one person that you can say 'thank you' to today?

LIFE APPLICATION

SAY: We should never let an opportunity pass without saying thank you. If we look around us, there is someone who needs to hear 'thank you' from you.

Wrap It Up

SAY: Be on the look-out for chances to say thank you to those people that God has brought you.

Chapter 73: God's Love Is So Sweet!

Scripture: What is love? It is not that we loved God. It is that he loved us and sent his Son to give his life to pay for our sins. – 1 John 4:10

Topic
Be Mine!

Purpose
To help children understand that God loves them and is calling them to be his.

Type:
Food

Supplies:

- Candy conversation hearts – large (Be sure they are the ones that have the messages – "Be Mine, I Love You, and Say Yes " on them)
- Optional: snack bags

Preparation

Pull out the hearts that say: I Love You, Be Mine, Say Yes. If you buy enough for the children to each take home a baggie with these 3 message hearts in it, then prepare these ahead of time.

PRESENTATION

SAY: Valentine's Day is just the sweetest day. Not only is it a day to show love to people we care about but there's lots of candy and other yummy treats that we enjoy to celebrate!

There are so many fun ways to celebrate love. Some people give flowers. Some people give balloons. Some people purchase candy.

STEP 1: Hold up a bag/box of conversational heart candies.

   SAY: These little candies can also help us learn about God's love.

STEP 2: Read 1 John 4:10.

   SAY: It says that God first loved us. *(Hold up the I LOVE YOU candy)* This candy says I love you. God showed his love for us that while we were still doing the wrong thing, he loved us. He loved us enough to send Jesus, his Son, to die

Take It Further

Connect this object lesson to other Bible passages:

- God is Love (1 John 4:8)
- Put on Love (Colossians 3:14)
- Love in Action (1 John 3:18)

on the cross for our sins so we could have a relationship with him.

STEP 3: Hold up the BE MINE candy.

SAY: God invites us to accept the gift of salvation. We need his forgiveness and guidance in our lives. We have to take the gift. He wants us to be his children.

STEP 4: Hold up the SAY YES candy.

SAY: When we say yes to God and pray for forgiveness. He forgives us, and we become children of God. We are in his forever family.

STEP 5: Depending on the group and response, you may want to continue with an opportunity to go deeper with small group leaders and see if anyone wants to accept the Lord.

STEP 6: Optional: Hand out the baggies of candy and encourage the children to use them to tell someone else the story of how God loves them. Be sure they can have a few pieces from a bowl, so they aren't tempted to eat their props.

DISCUSSION QUESTIONS

1. How did God show his love for us?
2. What does he want us to do?
3. If we are his children how can we tell him we love him?

LIFE APPLICATION

SAY: God's love is the best thing to remember on Valentine's Day. Take time to thank God for his love.

Wrap It Up

SAY: God knew our sin separated us from him. He loved us so much that he sent his Son to die for us. We have to accept that gift and Be HIS! If you have done this, take the time to thank God for the gift. If you have not, now is a good time to talk to someone about what you should do.

Chapter 74: Unconditional Love

Scripture: "May you have power together with all God's people to understand Christ's love. May you know how wide and long and high and deep it is."

– Ephesians 3:18

Topic
Big Love!

Purpose
To demonstrate that love does not have conditions.

Type:
Action

Supplies:

- List of "If, Then" statements

Preparation

Prepare a list of "If, Then" statements ahead of time, such as:

- If you love spaghetti, then rub your tummy.
- If you love football, then pretend you're throwing one.
- If you love school, then use your pointer finger to tap your forehead.
- If you love going on vacation, then jump up and down.
- If you love Jesus, then say, "I love Jesus!"

PRESENTATION

SAY: This week is Valentine's Day! It's the one day of the year where we remember to show special people in our life extra love. Sometimes we don't realize how important people are to us. This is a good time to think about it and make sure they know. Our Bible talks about something similar. Let's read.

STEP 1: Read Ephesians 3:18.

SAY: Wow, this reminds us that God's love is so great we cannot even grasp how big it is. We can do things to make God sad, but he will never stop loving us. This means his love for us is bigger than our actions. Let's do something fun.

STEP 2: Have the children stand on the far end of your presentation area.

SAY: When I call out a phrase, if it applies to you, do what it says.
- If you love spaghetti, then rub your tummy.
- If you love football, then pretend you're throwing one.
- If you love school, then use your pointer finger to tap your forehead.
- If you love going on vacation, then jump up and down.
- If you love Jesus, then say, "I love Jesus!"

Take It Further

Connect this object lesson to other Bible passages:

- True Love (1 Corinthians 13)
- Do Everything in Love (1 Corinthians 16:14)
- True and Pure (Philippians 4:8)

Object Lesson: Big Love!

STEP 3: Have them all sit down.

SAY: That was fun. You showed me what you loved by doing the action if you loved it. God shows us he loves us all the time. Can anyone tell me how God shows love? *(Allow answers)* Great answers. Just like you showed me what you loved by your actions, God shows us his love by all the things he does for us. The biggest way he showed us he loved us is by sending Jesus to the earth to live and die for our sins. God loves us as we are. He made us all unique, but the one thing we all have in common is each of us has sinned and need God's loving gift, Jesus.

DISCUSSION QUESTIONS

1. What does this verse tell about the love Jesus has for you?
2. When God shows love does it make you feel good?
3. How can we show God we love him?

LIFE APPLICATION

SAY: God loves us more than we can know. We can go through our day knowing that he is with us and caring for us.

Wrap It Up

SAY: No matter where we go or what we do, God's love for us will never leave.

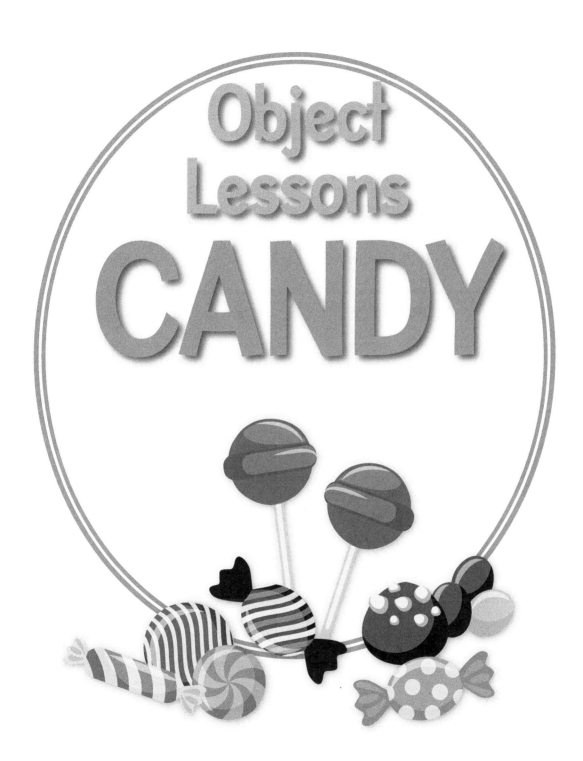

Chapter 75: Stretched Stronger

Scripture: "You will face all kinds of trouble. When you do, think of it as pure joy. Your faith will be put to the test. You know that when that happens it will produce in you the strength to continue." – James 1:2-3

Topic Tough Times

Purpose
To help children see challenges as a time to grow.

Type:
Everyday objects
Kid Volunteer

Supplies:
- Gummy worms

Preparation
None.

PRESENTATION

STEP 1: Hold up a gummy worm.

SAY: How many of you have had one of these? *(Allow answers)* They are chewy and soft. Have you ever tried to stretch one out? *(Allow answers)*

STEP 2: Stretch the gummy worm as long as you can.

SAY: I got pretty far before it broke. Does anyone want to see if they can stretch it farther? *(Allow volunteers to come up and try.)* Wow, some of you did better than me. But each of us took it past the breaking point. Sometimes we feel like we are being pulled out so far we will break. Have any of you ever felt like you have so many problems that upset you that you can't handle it anymore? *(Allow answers)*

Take It Further

Connect this object lesson to other Bible passages:
- God Is For Us (Romans 8:31)
- Our Struggle (Ephesians 6:12)
- More Than Conquerors (Romans 8:37)

Object Lesson: Tough Times

STEP 3: Read James 1:2-3

SAY: This says we are to be joyful when we have tough times! How can we do that? What do you think God means? *(Allow answers)* Well the answer is in that last part. It produces in us strength. When we go through something hard, it makes us stronger so that next time it is easier. God knows that if we live in a fallen world, bad things will happen. He wants us to be strong and ready for tough things. We should be happy that we are growing stronger ever time we have to go through something tough. God promises to go through it with us.

DISCUSSION QUESTIONS

1. Is there a situation in your life that seems hard to get through?
2. Can you think of a way going through it will make you stronger?
3. How can you let God get through it with you?

LIFE APPLICATION

SAY: It can be very easy to handle things on our own instead of waiting and allowing God to handle it for us. You do not fight battles alone. God is on your side.

Wrap It Up

SAY: Every time we go through a hard time, remember to be happy that God will use it to make you stronger.

CANDY – Hot Cinnamon Chewy Candy

Chapter 76: Hot Like Fire

Scripture: *"A gentle answer turns anger away. But mean words stir up anger."* – Proverbs 15:1

Type:
Food
Kid Volunteer

Supplies:
- Hot cinnamon chewy candies
- Oven mitt
- Sunscreen

Preparation

None.

Topic
Watch Your Words

Purpose
To demonstrate how, if we're not careful, our words or actions can hurt others.

PRESENTATION

SAY: Has anyone ever been burned? *(Allow answers)*

STEP 1: Hold up the oven mitt and the sunscreen.

SAY: What do these two things have in common? *(Allow answers)* That's right. This oven mitt and this bottle of sunscreen help protect us from getting burned. Burns are very painful, take a long time to heal and often leave a scar. Sometimes, the words we use or the way we treat people can be like a burn. They can hurt someone, cause relationships to become broken, and can leave behind a scar *(but we can't see that type of scar).* What causes that to happen? We don't always use the right words or treat people the way they should be treated. Our words or actions can sometimes be hurt as much as if we burned. Has anyone ever said something to you that hurt that much? *(Allow answers)*

Take It Further

Connect this object lesson to other Bible passages:
- Jonah's Anger (Jonah 4)
- Jacob and Esau (Genesis 25:19-34)
- Listening and Doing (James 1:19)

Object Lesson: Watch Your Words

STEP 2: Hold up the box of hot cinnamon chewy candies. Ask for a volunteer to try a candy.

SAY: How does that feel on your tongue? *(Allow answers)* I told you that eating one of these candies would burn your mouth, how many of you would want to eat them? *(Allow answers).* What if every time you said or did something to hurt someone you felt that burn on your tongue? *(Thank the child and have them sit down.)* That doesn't happen. Instead people just get hurt and then we have to fix it. God gives us instructions to follow to help us not have this happen.

STEP 3: Read Proverbs 15:1.

SAY: God knows that if we are gentle with our words and kind, we will not make people angry with us. We won't hurt them. But when we are mean, say bad things, gossip, or even lie, we stir up anger in others. The next time you eat something hot or sour, remember this verse. We want to use sweet or gentle words with others.

DISCUSSION QUESTIONS

1. When you think about your words and actions, would you say they mostly help or hurt people?
2. What makes our words or actions hurtful?
3. How can you remember to be more careful?

LIFE APPLICATION

SAY: At one time or another, all of us have used words or actions that have hurt someone. We can ask God to help us be more careful and aware of our words and actions and be someone who keeps the peace.

Wrap It Up

SAY: God wants us to use our words and actions to show love to others. When we don't, we can hurt feelings and damage relationships. We don't want our words (and actions) to be hot like fire; they should be gentle and loving.

Chapter 77: GRAND in the Hand

Scripture: *"Don't be controlled by love for money. Be happy with what you have."*
– Hebrews 13:5

Topic Contentment

Purpose
To illustrate that God wants us to be happy with what we already have.

Type:
Food

Supplies:
- Candy with money reference on cover (Chocolate, carmel, and crunchy cereal pieces)
- Piggy bank
- Wallet

Preparation

None.

PRESENTATION

STEP 1: Hold up the piggy bank for the children to see.

SAY: How many of you have one of these at home? *(Allow answers)* What do you use this for? *(Allow answers)* That's right, saving money. Saving money is a good thing. You might get money as an allowance, doing extra chores, Christmas gift or for your birthday and you might put some or all of it in a piggy bank. Maybe you have your eye on a new toy or video game and you need to save for it. But what happens when getting money (and a lot of it) becomes what's most important to you? Is that a good thing? *(Allow answers)*

STEP 2: Hold up your wallet.

SAY: What if I were to say I was going to give you $100,000? *(Hold up your wallet.)* How would you feel about that? *(Allow answers.)* You could do a lot with that! You could buy all kinds of toys

Take It Further

Connect this object lesson to other Bible passages:
- Treasures in Heaven (Matthew 6:19-21)
- The Prodigal Son (Luke 15:11-32)
- The Parable of the Rich Fool (Luke 12:13-21)

 Top 50 Object Lessons: Games & Activities

and cookies and potato chips and cool clothes with that much money! But there's only one problem - what if this is what I meant?

STEP 3: Show chocolate bar with money reference on it.

SAY: Some of you are probably disappointed about that. You probably were daydreaming about spending real money. When we focus on getting money and things, it starts to control our thoughts.

STEP 4: Read Hebrews 13:5.

SAY: This verse reminds us to pay attention to how important money and things become. God wants us to appreciate what we have and not focus on getting more of what we don't have.

DISCUSSION QUESTIONS

1. What is the favorite thing that you own?
2. Is that favorite thing more important to you than anything else?
3. Why do you think God wants us to be happy with what we have?

LIFE APPLICATION

SAY: When we begin to want more and more things, we can begin to focus on that more than we should. God wants us to be happy with what we already have.

Wrap It Up

SAY: We live in a time when people have a lot of stuff. We are blessed beyond measure to have more than we actually need. God wants us to be satisfied with what we already have and not strive to keep attaining more.

Chapter 78: God Sees the Heart

Scripture: The Lord does not look at the things people look at. People look at the outward appearance, but the Lord looks at what is in the heart.

– 1 Samuel 16:7b, NIV

Topic
Known by God

Purpose
To help children know that God sees who they really are.

Type:
Food

Supplies:
- Fruit shaped and flavored candy

Preparation
None

Optional Idea
Separate out one of each kind of the fruit flavors in the bag and use them with the kids to taste test. Have the kids vote on their favorite and see which flavor wins.

PRESENTATION

STEP 1: Hold up the bag of candy.

SAY: Can anyone tell me what these are? *(Allow answers)*

STEP 2: Pour the candy out on the table.

SAY: Wow, look at all those colors. These are all the colors of fruit. Look they are even shaped like the fruit. How many of you like the orange ones? *(Show of hands.)* How many of you like the yellow ones. *(Show of hands.)* *(This is where you would add the optional idea.)* I cannot stand the green ones. Do you think if these candies look like fruit they are made of fruit? *(Allow answers)* Hmm, let's find out. *(Read a few ingredients on the bag.)* Doesn't sound like fruit to me. So what it looks like is not what it really is.

STEP 3: Read 1 Samuel 16:7.

SAY: What do you think this means? *(Allow answers)* We only see what people show us. We draw conclusion by what we see. God can go past the outside of what people show us and see our heart. I am not talking about our physical heart. I am talking about who we really are, what we feel and think. You may be saying something nice to someone, but

Take It Further
Connect this object lesson to other Bible passages:
- Create in me a clean heart (Psalm 51:10)
- I knew you before I formed you (Jeremiah 1:5)
- You have examined my heart (Psalm 139:10)

Object Lesson: Known by God

thinking how much you don't like them inside. God knows what you really feel. We can't hide anything from God. But the same is true in reverse. People may think something bad about you that isn't true. God knows who you really are. Even if it seems people don't understand you, God does. He loves you and made you just the way you are.

DISCUSSION QUESTIONS

1. Can you remember a time you got to know someone and they weren't like you thought they would be?
2. Have you ever pretended to be something you aren't?
3. Do you think God knew the truth?

LIFE APPLICATION

SAY: God knows who you really are. He hears your thoughts and sees your heart. When you are with people, try to really get to know who they are and not judge them only by what you see.

Wrap It Up

SAY: It is important to remember that God made you just as you are. He loves who you are. Live your life showing who you really are.

CANDY – Twin Candy Bars
Chapter 79: **Double the Fun**

Scripture: "Carry each other's burdens, and in this way you will fulfill the law of Christ." – Galatians 6:2, NIV

Topic Community

Purpose
To remind children that sharing life together is better than going at it alone.

Type:
Everyday objects

Supplies:
- Package of candy with two bars
- Tray
- Things that come in pairs, such as:
  - Knife and fork (plastic)
  - Salt and pepper
  - Peanut butter and jelly
  - Pencil and paper

Preparation

Place the things that come in pairs on the tray. Place the tray on a table in front of your presentation area.

PRESENTATION

SAY: Some of my very favorite things come in a pair.

STEP 1: Show the pairs on your tray.

SAY: Look at all the things I have that we usually use together. Could we use each of the parts of these pairs alone? Can you use a knife without a fork? *(Allow answers)* Sure you can, but when you need to cut something, it helps to have the two work together. What about paper? Can you use a paper without a pencil? *(Allow answers)* Sure you can. You can make a paper airplane. However, when you use a paper and pencil together you can do so much more.

STEP 2: Read Galatians 6:2, NIV.

SAY: This verse teaches us that when we bring others into our life we are better, stronger. Each of the items on my tray are very different from each other. In our verse it is talking about finding other

Take It Further

Connect this object lesson to other Bible passages:
- Jacob and Esau (Genesis 25:19-34)
- Noah's Ark (Genesis 7:2)
- Two or More Gathered (Matthew 18:20)

people that believe like we do about God. When we have other believers standing with us in life we are stronger. It is more like this.

STEP 3: Open the candy with two bars.

SAY: When we are with people who have the same values and beliefs in God we are stronger and braver to stand up for the right things. We work together like all of these other pairs. (Point to the tray of pairs) We are able to tackle challenges with more back up, and help each other do what is right.

DISCUSSION QUESTIONS

1. Do you have another person in your life who believes like you do in God?
2. How can being with that person help you make better choices?
3. If you only have friends that don't believe in God, how can that cause problems?

LIFE APPLICATION

SAY: God gives us instructions to surround ourselves with people who are in our faith community to help us be strong.

Wrap It Up

SAY: Today we saw things that work well on their own but really shine when they are paired up with something else. When we share life together in community, we are able to support each other and help each other when needed.

CANDY – Round Sucker w/ Soft Center

Chapter 80: Crushing Sin

Scripture: But your sins have separated you from your God. – Isaiah 59:2a

Topic
Sin Separates

Purpose
To help children recognize that sin separates us from God.

Type:
Messy

Supplies:
- Round sucker with soft center
- Hammer or something that can crush a sucker
- Towel of any kind or size

Preparation
Place hammer, sucker, and towel on the table by where you will teach.

PRESENTATION

STEP 1: Hold up the sucker.

SAY: How many of you have had one of these before? *(Allow answers)* What is in the center? That is right, the soft candy center. When I see this, it reminds me of our hearts. Before we become Christians and we sin, it is just like this candy that surrounds the center. Slowly but surely sin surrounds our heart. As time goes by, it is harder for God to get to our heart. We have a more difficult time believing and hearing God. God warns us in the Bible about this.

STEP 2: Read Isaiah 59:2a.

SAY: That separation is eternal. It goes on forever. God didn't want that. He made a way through all those layers and layers of sin.

STEP 3: Get out the hammer. Place the sucker on the towel. *(Wait to*

Take It Further

Connect this object lesson to other Bible passages:
- Can anyone hide in secret places (Jeremiah 23:24)
- For all have sinned and fall short (Romans 3:23)
- If we confess our sins, He is faithful (1 John 1:9)

 Top 50 Object Lessons: Games & Activities

hit the candy until instructed to.) You can either smash the candy without covering it with the towel so that the pieces go flying for effect or cover it over before hitting it to contain the pieces.

SAY: *(Holding up the hammer)* God knew our sin separated us from him. He wanted us in a relationship with him forever. He sent his Son, Jesus, to die on a cross for our sins. When Jesus died on the cross he became the hammer. This hammer just stays right here ready to free our hearts from sin. When you ask Jesus into your heart he *(bring down the hammer and smash the sucker)* crushes through all that sin and makes it possible for us to connect with God. When we ask God to forgive us he removes all the sin from our life. We start with a clean slate. No hardened candy shell. Just a soft heart that can now be in a relationship with God.

DISCUSSION QUESTIONS

1. Why does doing the wrong things separate us from God?

2. How can we connect with God if we do wrong things?

3. What happens if you keep doing wrong things after you become a Christian?

LIFE APPLICATION

SAY: When we pray for forgiveness, God breaks through the sin and makes it possible for us to have a relationship with him.

Wrap It Up

SAY: We have to ask for forgiveness and accept Jesus' gift of salvation to have a relationship with God. When Jesus died on the cross he made it possible to have sin crushed so we could be with God forever.

Chapter 81: Filled with God

Scripture: God created mankind in his own image, in the image of God he created them; male and female he created them. – Genesis 1:27, NIV

Topic
Made in His Image

Purpose
To help children realize that they are made in the image of God.

Type:
Food

Supplies:
- Candy coated chocolate in different colors
- Bowl

Preparation
None

PRESENTATION

STEP 1: Pour the candy into a bowl.

SAY: Everyone knows what these are. Let's talk about them for a minute. I love all the colors. They come in so many different colors. Did you know you can actually go online and find this kind of candy in even more colors than this to choose from. That reminds me of us. We all come from different cultures and backgrounds. Most of us have a different shade of skin from each other. We are good at different things. But when you take off this outer shell, *(break one open)* they are all the same inside. They are all filled with the same thing.

STEP 2: Read Genesis 1:27.

SAY: In this verse God tells us that we are each made in his image. He has poured into each of us a spirit that is connected and resembles him. We are filled with God's

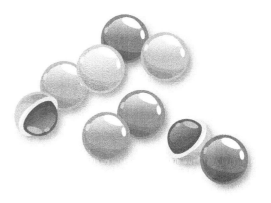

Take It Further

Connect this object lesson to other Bible passages:
- There are different kinds of gifts, but the same Spirit (1 Corinthians 12:4-6)
- Made in God's likeness (James 3:9)
- ...Between Greek and Jew... Christ is in all (Colossians 3:11)

love. If you think about it, without that love in us, we are fragile and easily broken like the delicate outer shell of this candy. Without God's love in us we would be empty.

STEP 3: Pass out a small handful of candy to each child.

SAY: From now on, when you see these candies, remember that even though we are all unique, God has made us the same in that we are made in his image. Without God in our hearts we are fragile and easily broken.

DISCUSSION QUESTIONS

1. How many differences can you see in the people around us right now?

2. Do we all act like we are filled with God?

3. How should we behave knowing we are made in God's image?

LIFE APPLICATION

SAY: When you meet people who are different from you, remember that they are like you in that they are filled with God's love and made in his image.

Wrap It Up

SAY: People are so different. God wants us to remember that we are all made in his image. We should focus on that and not our differences.

Chapter 82: Exploding Joy

Scripture: "Always be joyful because you belong to the Lord. I will say it again. Be joyful." – Philippians 4:4

Topic
Live Joyfully

Purpose
Help children see they should live joyfully.

Type:
Food
Kid Volunteer

Supplies:
- Fizzy Rock Candy
- Old cup container

Preparation

None.

PRESENTATION

STEP 1: Hold up the package of fizzy rock candy.

SAY: Has anyone ever tried these? *(Allow answers)* Can someone tell me what happens when you put them in your mouth? *(Allow answers)* It is an explosive reaction. You can't stop it. Does anyone want to try it? *(Pour a few into a few hands and let them try it.)* It reminds me of a Bible story.

STEP 2: Hold up the old cup.

SAY: The Bible tells in Acts, the story of a man who was unable to walk since he was born. Back then the only hope they had was for family to care for them or to beg. This man had to beg by the gate of the city. He probably had some old can that he held out to allow people to drop coins in. One day the apostles Peter and John were about to pass him. The beggar called out for money. Peter and John helped heal him instead, through the power of God. They grabbed his hand and he stood up for the first time in his life! What happened next reminds me of the fizzy rocks. He walked and jumped and praised God! We can understand why this man was so joyful, but God tells us that knowing who Jesus is and what he did for us, should make us this joyful all the time.

Take It Further

Connect this object lesson to other Bible passages:
- Wise men rejoiced with great joy (Matthew 2:10-11)
- Disciples were filled with joy (Acts 13:49, 52)
- May the God of hope fill you with joy (Romans 15:13)

Object Lesson:
Live Joyfully

STEP 3: Read Philippians 4:4.

SAY: Paul was writing to the people of Philippi. He loved them and knew they were doing good things for God. He knew they faced challenges because of their faith in God. Paul reminded them to always live their life joyful! With joy exploding out of them with enthusiasm like the fizzy rocks in our mouth. We have so much to be happy about. Jesus has made a way for us to live forever with God.

DISCUSSION QUESTIONS

1. When was the last time your felt joyful? What was the reason?
2. Why would thinking about having a relationship with God make us JOYFUL?
3. How can we remind ourselves to live joyfully?

LIFE APPLICATION

SAY: Live each day remembering what Jesus has done for us and live with explosive joy!

Wrap It Up

SAY: God has made a way for us to be with him forever. He sacrificed his son for the payment of our sins. When thinking of this sacrifice, we are to live life full of joy!

Chapter 83: Inside Out

Scripture: "Therefore, if anyone is in Christ, the new creation has come: The old has gone, the new is here!"
– 2 Corinthians 5:17, NIV

Topic
New Life

Purpose
To help children know that when they become a Christian they are new.

Type:
Food

Supplies:
- 1 pack of 4 Peanut Butter Cups
- Solid chocolate candy
- Plastic knife
- 4 dessert-sized paper plates

Preparation

Put one uncut peanut butter cup on a plate. Cut the other 3 in half, then push them back together so you can't see the inside, place on a plate. Put plates in your presentation area.

**CAUTION:
BE AWARE OF ANY PEANUT ALLERGIES!**
(Some children can't even be in the same room with peanuts) Be sure to inform the parents of this activity before doing it.

PRESENTATION

SAY: Sometimes, things are not what they appear. They can look one way but really be another. Take this piece of chocolate, for instance.

STEP 1: Hold up the plate containing the whole, uncut peanut butter cup. If necessary, take it closer to the children so that they can see it.

SAY: When we look at this piece of chocolate, it looks like a yummy piece of chocolate. When we smell it, it smells like a yummy piece of chocolate. However, when we dig a little deeper, we'll realize there is something different going on inside.

STEP 2: Hold up a plate containing the halved peanut butter cups. Separate the cups so that the children can see the peanut butter inside. Pass around the other plates of halved cups so that children can get a closer look.

Take It Further

Connect this object lesson to other Bible passages:
- Darkness Brought to Light (Luke 8:17)
- Judas Betrays Jesus (Luke 22)
- True Love (1 Corinthians 13)

Object Lesson: New Life

SAY: These pieces of chocolate remind us that things on the inside don't always match what's on the outside. In the case of this chocolate, that's not a bad thing, especially if you like to eat chocolate and peanut butter together. But in other cases, it's not good if the inside doesn't match the outside.

STEP 3: Read 2 Corinthians 5:17.

SAY: If we say we love God, but have not turned our life over to him yet, we are like these candies. We say we are one thing on the outside, but nothing is different on the inside. When we ask Jesus to forgive us of our sins, and become Christians, we are changed inside. We are a new creation.

STEP 4: Cut open the solid chocolate candy.

SAY: When we say we love God and do our best to follow him and what the Bible says, we are like this candy. We live out our life honestly. What people hear us say and do, is the truth. We really are trying to be like Jesus on the inside and outside and do the right things. Let's all be like these candies. *(Hold up the solid chocolate.)*

STEP 5: Hand out little pieces of solid chocolate for the kids to eat.

DISCUSSION QUESTIONS

1. Have you become a Christian?
2. Do you live your life like a new creation?
3. Can people tell you are a Christian by your actions? Which actions show this?

LIFE APPLICATION

SAY: If people know that you love Jesus but your actions show otherwise, that is a problem. What's on the inside should match what's on the outside.

Wrap It Up

SAY: When you love Jesus, people around you should be able to tell by looking at the outside. They should be able to see something different about you - on the inside and the outside.

Top 50 Object Lessons: Games & Activities

Chapter 84: Promise Keeper

Scripture: "God isn't a mere man. He can't lie. He isn't a human being. He doesn't change his mind. He speaks, and then he acts. He makes a promise, and then he keeps it." – Numbers 23:19, NIRV

Topic
Promises

Purpose
To help children understand that God keeps his promises.

Type:
Food

Supplies:
- Rainbow colored candies
- Bowl (optional)

Preparation
None.

PRESENTATION

SAY: Who can tell me what a promise is? *(Allow answers)* That's right, a promise is when a person says they'll do something and they actually do it. We should all strive to be people who keep our promises because when we don't, people won't trust us. They can't rely on us.

STEP 1: Read Numbers 23:19.

> **SAY:** This verse reminds us when God makes a promise, he keeps it. That means that we can believe what he says. He is trustworthy, which means we can trust him. God's promises are given to us to comfort us as we face each day. It also talks about how hard it is for humans to do what we should. Sometimes we take how hard something is for us and think of God the same way. God isn't like us. He is holy. He says something to us and we can count on it to be true.

STEP 2: Pour the rainbow candies into a bowl.

> **SAY:** When I see these different colored candies, it reminds me of a promise God made. Can anyone guess which promise? *(Allow answers if they aren't getting it, say these RAINBOW colored candies)* That's right, the rainbow is a sign of a promise

Take It Further
Connect this object lesson to other Bible passages:
- God Doesn't Change (Malachi 3:6)
- Jesus Comforts His Disciples (John 14:1-3)
- Keep Your Word (James 5:12)

 Top 50 Object Lessons: Games & Activities

Object Lesson: Promises

from God. What Bible story was that from? *(Allow answers- Noah's Ark)* That's right, Noah's Ark. After the flood, God promised to never flood the whole earth again. Every time you see a rainbow, remember that God keeps his promises. We can trust him with our lives.

STEP 2: Pick up and pour candies through your hands to draw the children's eyes.

SAY: Every time you see these candies I want you to remember that God is trustworthy. When he makes a promise, he keeps it. When you read the Bible and you see he is making a promise, you know you can count on him.

DISCUSSION QUESTIONS

1. Has anyone ever broken a promise to you?
2. How did that feel?
3. How can you be more trustworthy and keep your promises like God?

LIFE APPLICATION

SAY: As humans, we fail each other because we're not perfect. God will never fail us because he is holy. He will keep every promise that he has ever made.

Wrap It Up

SAY: We can believe God's promises to us because he has kept every single promise. He is not one to say one thing and then do another. He will do just as he says he will.

Chapter 85: **Eyes on the Prize**

Scripture: "I press on toward the goal to win the prize for which God has called me heavenward in Christ Jesus." – Philippians 3:14, NIV

Topic
Stay Focused

Purpose
To demonstrate how important it is to keep your eyes focused on what's in front of you.

Type:
Action,
Kid Volunteer

Supplies:
- Paddle balls

Preparation
None.

PRESENTATION

STEP 1: Start playing with a paddle board. Do a bad job playing with it.

SAY: Oh dear, I don't think I will ever get the hang of this game. *(Keep trying and trying)* Does anyone have any suggestions on how to get better at this? *(Allow answers)* Do we have any paddleball players here today? *(Show of hands)*

STEP 2: Invite a few children up to play with the paddle balls you have. (If they are unsure how to use them, give them a quick tutorial.) After playing, have the participants return to their seats.

SAY: Wow, some of you got the hang of that real quick, and some of you had to work on it a bit. What are some important things you do to become good at doing something? *(Allow answers)* Those are some great responses! While it takes many skills to help you become good at something, one of the most important is

Take It Further

Connect this object lesson to other Bible passages:
- Jesus Calms the Storm (Mark 4:35-41)
- Focus Your Mind (Colossians 3:2)
- Stay Focused (Proverbs 4:25)

knowing the goal and keeping your eyes on the goal. Our paddleball players knew that the goal was to hit the ball using the paddle. They had to keep their eye on the ball so that they knew where to swing the paddle.

STEP 3: Read Philippians 3:14.

SAY: The verse says, "I press on toward the goal". That "I" means it is our job to work at doing the right things. The goal is to be in heaven with God someday and to try to be like Jesus along the way. When it says, "press on", this tells us that it can be a challenge and we should not give up. We are to press on even when it is hard.

STEP 4: Play the paddle board again and each time you do it get better. *(If you are not able to do it well, then just point out which child did do it well and say the same thing.)*

SAY: The paddle board was a good example of how important it is to keep our eyes on the goal we're trying to reach. If we don't know the goal *(Because we don't read the Bible)* or we take our eyes off the goal, *(by focusing on other things besides God)* we might not hit the target. If we press on, we can make our goal, to be like Jesus.

DISCUSSION QUESTIONS

1. Do you find it easy to focus on what's ahead or are you more easily distracted?
2. What goals or challenges have you set for yourself?
3. What can you do to press on in trying to be more like Jesus?

LIFE APPLICATION

SAY: We are all capable of growing to be more Christ like when we set our minds to it, with God's help. We have to decide to do it and stay focused on Jesus.

Wrap It Up

SAY: Spending time in the Bible and learning about what God wants us to do, will help us be more like Jesus. Sometimes it will be hard, but God can help you press on.

Chapter 86: All Mixed Up

Scripture: And we know that in all things God works for the good of those who love him, who have been called according to his purpose.
– Romans 8:28, NIV

Topic
Trust God

Purpose
To demonstrate how we can trust God, even when we don't know his plan.

Type:
Action

Supplies:
- 3 different puzzles with the same amount of pieces – low piece count so it doesn't take too long

Preparation
Take all the puzzle pieces out of each box, and place in the wrong box (the puzzle pieces should not match the picture on the front of the box).
Set the puzzles in three spots around the room where the kids can assemble them in groups.

PRESENTATION

SAY: On a rainy day, I love to put puzzles together. I love dumping out all of the pieces and try to begin putting it together. It can be hard but when it's all put together, I feel very good about what I've accomplished. Maybe you like to put puzzles together. Maybe you like to put other things together, like building bricks or model cars or robots. There's something about using your hands to create something.

STEP 1: Divide the children into three groups and have them go to one of the puzzles.

STEP 2: Give each group a boxed puzzle to put together. Instruct them to use the picture on the front of the box to put the puzzle together. *(After a few minutes, the children may begin to complain that something isn't quite right but encourage them to keep going.)*

SAY: What was challenging about this task? *(Allow answers),* So, you thought the picture showed you how the puzzle would turn out? I see.

STEP 3: Send the children back to their original seats.

Take It Further

Connect this object lesson to other Bible passages:
- Formed by God (Psalm 139:13-16)
- Peace in God (1 Thessalonians 5:23-24)
- Our Plans vs God's Purpose (Proverbs 19:21)

Object Lesson:
Trust God

SAY: When we have the right picture, we can see how all the pieces of a puzzle fit together. God has the real picture of our life. He sees how everything that happens fits together for good. We cannot see the whole picture. When things happen in our life we don't like, or are confusing to us, we think something is wrong. But God has a plan for us that is good.

STEP 4: Read Romans 8:28.

SAY: God has planned out our life. He wants good things for us. Knowing that God is in control helps when hard things happen. We can have hope that all things will work out okay, because God is in control. Remember when you were putting the puzzles together, the pieces still fit into place with each other. You just weren't able to completely understand how because you didn't have to right picture. You can trust that God has the right picture. Anything that happens is allowed by God for your good. You have a safe future in him.

DISCUSSION QUESTIONS

1. Is it hard for you to trust God? Why or why not?
2. Do you like to plan or do you like to 'go with the flow'?
3. What is one way that you can trust God with the unknown this week?

LIFE APPLICATION

SAY: It's easy to trust when we see what's ahead and know what to expect but it's harder to trust when we don't know. We can trust God because he is trustworthy and has our best interest at heart.

Wrap It Up

SAY: When confusing or difficult things happen to you, pray that God will help you see his perfect love and plan for you. Go through challenges knowing you will grow and learn from them.

DISCOUNT STORE – Water Bottle

Chapter 87: So Refreshing

Scripture: "...Let anyone who is thirsty come to me and drink. Whoever believes in me, as Scripture has said, rivers of living water will flow from within them."
– John 7:37-38, NIV

Topic
Living Water

Purpose
To explain how the water Jesus offers is the most refreshing water we'll ever need.

Type:
Everyday objects

Supplies:
- Bottle of clean water
- Bottle of dirty water
- Backpack

Preparation

Place the bottles of water inside of the backpack. Wear the backpack when you enter the presentation area.

PRESENTATION

STEP 1: Enter your presentation area by jogging or quickly walking in. Pretend as though you're out of breath as you talk.

SAY: I went for a quick jog (or walk) and boy, it has made me so thirsty! Have you ever been so thirsty that you could drink just about anything? *(Allow answers).* Right now, I need something refreshing.

STEP 2: Stop and take the backpack off. Pull out the two bottles of water and place on a table or floor side by side.

SAY: Now, I need a refreshing drink, one that will quench my thirst. Which one would you choose? *(Hold up each bottle and then allow answers.)* Why? *(Allow answers)* Okay, I understand.

STEP 3: Read John 7:37-38.

SAY: This tells us that Jesus is like clean, living water flowing out of us. When we go to Jesus to learn about life

Take It Further
Connect this object lesson to other Bible passages:
- The Woman at the Well (John 4:1-26)
- Well-Watered Garden (Isaiah 58:11)
- Refresh, Refreshed (Proverbs 11:25)

 Top 50 Object Lessons: Games & Activities

and live the right way, it is like a refreshing, clean drink.

STEP 4: Hold up dirty bottle of water.

SAY: So you think that this bottle is dirty and might make me sick? *(Allow answers)* Did you know you may be drinking dirty water every day? When we try to follow what we see on TV, or things people do, or what the world shows us we should be, it is like drinking filthy water. This verse tells us that Jesus is 'living water'. We should only believe in him and follow what he wants us to do. Otherwise, we are filling our lives with dirty, unhealthy things.

DISCUSSION QUESTIONS

1. What do you think Jesus meant when he said "rivers of living water will flow from within them"?
2. How might Jesus be like living water to us?
3. What is one way that you can rely on Jesus to refresh you this week?

LIFE APPLICATION

SAY: We need to choose to believe in Jesus and follow him. When we do, he will send the Holy Spirit to refresh us like a clean cool drink of water.

Wrap It Up

SAY: When we believe in Jesus he comes into our life and cleans it out. Then when we behave like Jesus it is like he is flowing out of us.

Chapter 88: Peaceful Flight

Scripture: How can a young person keep his life pure? By living in keeping with your Word.
– Psalm 119:9

Topic
Peace

Purpose
To help kids understand that Jesus is our peace in the storms of life.

Type:
Everyday objects

Supplies:
- Kite

Preparation
Make sure the kite is assembled with a string. If possible, arrange for the kite to be hung in the corner of the room and the string to reach down to where you will be.

PRESENTATION

SAY: A windy day is a great day for doing some fun activities that might not work if it wasn't windy. One of those activities is kite flying. How many of you have ever flown a kite? *(Allow answers)* Kite flying is great on a windy day.

STEP 1: Point to the kite up in the corner or hold it up.

SAY: What do you need to fly a kite? *(Allow answers)* That's right. You need wind, and to be outside. You need a small tail of material on the end and you need a string.

STEP 2: Hold up the string.

SAY: What would happen if you tried to fly your kite without a string? *(Allow answers)* Well you would have a hard time getting it up. What if we got the kite up in the air and the string came off. *(Allow answers)* It would be out of control. Let's imagine that this kite is us. The wind is all the different choices and directions you can go. You are out in life making choices attached to this string. The string is God's Word, the Bible.

STEP 3: Pick up the Bible and read Psalm 119:9.

Take It Further
Connect this object lesson to other Bible passages:
- Jesus Calms the Storm (Matthew 8:23-27)
- Daniel in the Lion's Den (Daniel 6)
- Joshua Becomes Israel's Leader (Joshua 1)

Object Lesson: Peace

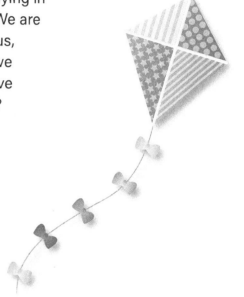

SAY: When we follow what the Bible tells us, we are staying in God's will. We are following his way and his guidance. We are flying through life and God's Word has a good hold on us, helping us make good choices. What would happen if we are the kite, and we cut the string? *(Allow answers)* Have you ever seen a kite flying high, cut loose from a string? It plummets to the ground. The wind grabs it and does whatever it wants with it. Life will grab ahold of you if you don't have God's Word to guide you.

DISCUSSION QUESTIONS

1. Do you ever read the Bible?
2. How can reading the Bible make your life better?
3. Do you ever feel like you are not making good choices?

LIFE APPLICATION

SAY: When you take the time to be in the Bible, God can direct your life. You will be able to do the right thing and keep your life pure.

Wrap It Up

SAY: Get in the habit of reading your Bible and following God's way. When you do no matter what challenges come along, God will have ahold of you and will keep you safe.

Chapter 89: Light in the Darkness

Scripture: "Jesus spoke to the people again. He said, 'I am the light of the world. Those who follow me will never walk in darkness. They will have have the light that leads to life.'" – John 8:12, NIRV

Topic
Light of the World

Purpose
To help children understand that Jesus wants us to be his light in a dark world.

Type:
Action

Supplies:
- 4 highlighters
- 4 copies of a Bible word search (4 of the same)

Preparation

None

PRESENTATION

STEP 1: Divide the group into four groups.

STEP 2: Distribute a highlighter and word search puzzle to each group.

SAY: I want each group to look for as many Bible words as you can find in 3 minutes. Get ready, GO!

STEP 3: After the 3-5 minutes have passed, bring the group back together.

SAY: You all did a great job with the word search puzzle! How many words did each group find? *(Allow answers).* I could have given you a pencil, a pen, a marker, or a crayon to use to circle the words you found, but I wanted you to use a highlighter. Do you have any guesses why? *(Allow answers)* Highlighters help words stand out on a page. They make words easy to find on a page.

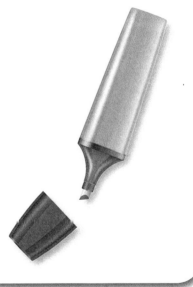

Take It Further

Connect this object lesson to other Bible passages:
- Let Your Light Shine (Matthew 5:16)
- Children of the Light (Ephesians 5:8)
- The Lord is My Light (Psalm 27:1)

In many ways, those who believe in Jesus are like highlighters. We stand out like brightly-colored words. That's because the light of Jesus is inside of us.

STEP 4: Read John 8:12.

SAY: When we have Jesus in our life and we are following his ways, we show others who Jesus is to us, and how he has changed us. That is what it means when it says we will have the light of Jesus in us. So just like the highlighter shows people where to find the Bible words on the page, we help people find Jesus when we follow him.

DISCUSSION QUESTIONS

1. What are some ways that you can tell that someone loves Jesus?

2. Do you think that people who love Jesus look different?

3. How can people see the light of Jesus in you?

LIFE APPLICATION

SAY: When we believe in Jesus, we grow in our relationship with him by reading our Bibles, praying, and studying him. By studying him, we begin to be like him. He wants us to be his light in a dark world.

Wrap It Up

SAY: Being the light of Jesus in a dark world means that we are kind, forgiving, generous loving, people who model what Jesus modeled in the Bible. Don't be afraid to be a shining light for Jesus!

Chapter 90: Second Chance

Scripture: *"God, create a pure heart in me. Give me a new spirit that is faithful to you."*
– Psalm 51:10

Topic
Pure Heart

Purpose
To illustrate how when God forgives us, we are given a second chance.

Type:
Everyday objects

Supplies:
- Bottle of White Liquid Paper
- Easel
- Easel Pad
- Black permanent marker

Preparation
Set the easel pad on the easel and place the easel in the front of your presentation area. On the easel pad, draw a heart and write "Sinner" in it.

PRESENTATION

SAY: When you write with a pencil and you make a mistake, what do you do? *(Allow answers)* That's right. You erase it with an eraser. Some mistakes are not so easy to erase. Can we erase something that we have done wrong?

STEP 1: Stand by the poster on the easel.

SAY: The Bible tells us that we are all born with sin in our hearts and are separated from God. The good news is that because Jesus died on the cross for our sins, we now have a way to be with God. Can anyone tell me what that is? *(Allow answers)* That's right. When we become Christians, we pray and ask Jesus to forgive us of our sins, and make us part of God's forever family.

STEP 2: Begin to paint the white out over the words.

Take It Further

Connect this object lesson to other Bible passages:
- Sins Removed (Psalm 103:12)
- Confess and Be Forgiven (1 John 1:9)
- Out With the Old, In With the New (2 Corinthians 5:17)

SAY: When we do that it is like taking a bottle of white out and erasing the sin from our hearts. God removes it, erases it and remembers it no more. We are forgiven.

STEP 3: Read Psalm 51:10.

SAY: When we are forgiven God creates in us a pure, clean heart. *(Point to the blotted out word in the heart.)* We should be so grateful that we want to do what he says. That is what it means when the writer asks God to give him a new spirit that is faithful. To be faithful means to follow and obey God. We need to realize that God has done an amazing thing for us. He has provided a way for us to be with him, forgiven us, and given us a new heart and a new life. We should want to do all he asks of us.

DISCUSSION QUESTIONS

1. What does it mean to be forgiven?
2. How do you feel about being forgiven by God?
3. How does being forgiven by God affect how you forgive others?

LIFE APPLICATION

SAY: When God forgives us, he gives us a second chance. We have a clean start, a pure heart.

Wrap It Up

SAY: When we ask God to forgive us, he can give us a new life. We need to live our life faithfully.

Chapter 91: Growing in Faith

Scripture: "Have your roots in him. Build yourselves up in him. Grow strong in what you believe, just as you were taught. Be more thankful than ever before."
– Colossians 2:7

**Topic
Growing With Jesus**

Purpose
To help children understand that a relationship with Jesus should be a growing relationship.

Type:
Everyday objects

Supplies:
- 1 or 2 small plants
- Garden gloves
- Potting soil
- Pitcher of water

Preparation
Set the plants, garden gloves, potting soil, and water pitcher on a table in the front of the presentation area.

PRESENTATION

STEP 1: Put on the garden gloves and manipulate the potting soil as you talk.

SAY: I love plants! I love taking care of them and helping them be beautiful, healthy, and strong. What kinds of things do plants need to grow healthy and strong? *(Allow answers)* That's right! Giving them the right amount of sunlight, water, and fertilizer helps them to have deep roots so they grow the way they're supposed to.

STEP 2: Take a plant out of a pot and show the children the roots.

SAY: Look at all the roots on this plant. Each one of them reaches out into the soil. The roots grab the water and nutrition from the soil and give it to the plant to grow. God does the same with us. When we have a relationship with him he helps us grow by giving us his Holy Spirit, his Bible, and good people in our lives to teach and guide us.

STEP 3: Repot the plant and give it some water.

SAY: The more we are praying, reading the Bible, and going to church the deeper our understanding and love of God will grow.

Take It Further

Connect this object lesson to other Bible passages:
- Grow in Grace and Knowledge (2 Peter 3:18)
- Grow to Become the Body of Christ (Ephesians 4:15)
- Young Faith (1 Timothy 4:12)

Object Lesson:
Growing With Jesus

STEP 4: Read Colossians 2:7.

SAY: Listen to these words. Your roots, build yourselves, you believe, and you were taught. What do they all have in common? *(Allow answers)* That's right, the word you. We have to take part in this relationship with God. We have to make the effort to grow close to God. When we get so busy we don't take time to pray, read the Bible, and go to church to learn, we don't grow.

DISCUSSION QUESTIONS

1. Would you say that you are growing in your relationship with Jesus?

2. How are you growing in your relationship with Jesus?

3. Is there anything you need to do more or less of to know Jesus better?

LIFE APPLICATION

SAY: Giving the plant what it needs, will help it to grow healthy and strong. Our relationship with Jesus should be a growing relationship. Take the time to pray, worship, and read your Bible.

Wrap It Up

SAY: God wants us to be in a relationship with him, the type of relationship where we know him personally. Do you have that kind of relationship with him, one that's growing?

Chapter 92: Don't Keep it to Yourself

Scripture: "Come, follow me," Jesus said, "and I will send you out to fish for people."
– Matthew 4:19, NIV

Topic
Tell Others

Type:
Kid-Volunteer

Purpose
To illustrate how Jesus wants us to invite others to follow him.

Supplies:

- Toy fishing set (poles with magnetic ends)
- 8 index cards
- 8 paper clips
- Black marker
- Bucket

Preparation

Use the marker to write the following on the index cards: Rich people; poor people; men; women; old people; young people; people who look like us; people who don't look like us. Then attach a paper clip to one end of each index card.

PRESENTATION

SAY: What is usually the first thing we do when we get something new? *(Allow answers)* Usually, we tell other people about it and we show them what the new thing is! We can't keep the good news to ourselves. We want everyone to know and see! Jesus wants everyone we meet to hear about him and the wonderful ways that he loves us. He wants the news to be so great that we share it with everyone! The Bible tells us how Jesus called his followers (who were fishermen) to leave everything behind and become 'fishers of men.'

STEP 1: Read Matthew 4:19.

SAY: So what do you think Jesus wanted his disciples to do? *(Allow answers)* That's right. He wanted them to tell others about him so that they could live with him forever. Let's find out who Jesus might want to know about him.

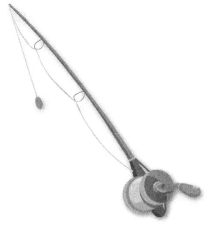

Take It Further

Connect this object lesson to other Bible passages:
- Great Commission (Matthew 28:19)
- Deny Yourself and Take Up Your Cross (Matthew 16:24)
- Receiving Power (Acts 1:8)

STEP 2: Call up several volunteers (one for each fishing pole you have) and give them a fishing pole. Place the index cards in the bucket.

SAY: There are many, many people who need to hear how much Jesus loves them. I am going to have these friends *(point to the volunteers)* fish for people and read their card to us to answer the question: Who needs to hear about Jesus's love?

STEP 3: One at a time, have the volunteers 'fish' for a card and read what's written on it. After all cards have been selected, collect the fishing poles and have the volunteers return to their seats.

SAY: The news of Jesus is so great we should be telling everyone. You can see that all kinds of people in your life need to hear about him.

DISCUSSION QUESTIONS

1. Have you ever shared about Jesus with someone?
2. How did you feel when you shared - happy, scared, excited?
3. Who is one person that you can share Jesus with this week?

LIFE APPLICATION

SAY: When we have good news, we share it. Sharing about Jesus is the best news we can share. Jesus wants us to invite others to follow him so that they can live with him forever.

Wrap It Up

SAY: Inviting others to follow Jesus takes courage but Jesus will give us the courage we need. Sharing his love with others is what he commands us to do. He doesn't want us to keep it to ourselves!

Chapter 93: Community Table

Scripture: "The believers studied what the apostles taught. They shared life together. They broke bread and ate together. And they prayed."
– Acts 2:42, NIRV

Topic Togetherness

Purpose
To illustrate how God wants us to live life in community with others.

Type:
Kid-Volunteer

Supplies:
- Plastic table cloth
- 4-8 of each of the following: paper plates, cups, napkins, eating utensils
- Table and chairs
- Centerpiece and candles (optional)

Preparation
Set the table in advance of your presentation. If desired, you can set up more than one table so that all children can have a spot at the table. You could also serve a snack or light meal if you choose.

PRESENTATION

STEP 1: Stand over by the set table.

SAY: Sometimes, when a table is set like this *(point to the set table)*, it could mean that a holiday or a special meal with friends is about to take place. For some people, it could mean that it's time to reconnect with your family after a busy day apart.

STEP 2: Invite a few volunteers up to have a seat at the table.

SAY: What kinds of things do you talk about at the table with friends or family?

STEP 3: Have them share what kinds of things they talk about at their tables at home. Then have them return to their seats.

SAY: In addition to a delicious meal, stories are often shared around the table – stories about our day, our feelings, what's happening in the world. The stories shared around the table help bring us closer to those we're seated with.

STEP 4: Hold up the Bible.

SAY: Many stories in the Bible took place around a table. I don't think God wanted people to sit at the table to simply eat.

Take It Further

Connect this object lesson to other Bible passages:
- The Lord's Supper (Luke 22:7-38)
- Let's Keep Meeting (Hebrews 10:25)
- Everyday Life (Acts 2:46)

I think he wanted them to be in fellowship with each other and be positioned to learn. He wanted them to learn something.

STEP 5: Read Acts 2:42.

SAY: When the earliest church was started, people did church in homes and many conversations took place around the table. Those conversations helped them to grow in their faith and get to know each other better. The next time you are sitting around a table with your family, share your day and listen to what everyone has to say.

DISCUSSION QUESTIONS

1. Who is usually seated around your table at home?
2. What do you normally talk about?
3. How might the conversations you have at the table help you to know each other better?

LIFE APPLICATION

SAY: When the early church started, they lived in community. They shared everything they had, even meals around the table. God wants us to live life in community with others who believe in Jesus. He doesn't want us to live alone.

Wrap It Up

SAY: Think about conversations you have at the table. Some are good and funny. Some are sad and more serious. Either way, when we share meals and conversation with people, we open up our heart to others, which is what living in community is all about.

Topic Index

Bible Story / Verse Index

Type Index

More RoseKidz Books

Check Out These Great Titles!

Teach the best 50 lessons from the popular *Instant Bible Lessons* series. *The Top 50 Instant Bible Lessons for Preschoolers* includes quick and easy-to-use resources for Sunday-school teachers with reproducible hand-outs, arts and crafts templates, puzzles, games, and step-by-step instructions. Ages two to five years.

ISBN: 9781628624977

More great lessons from the popular *Instant Bible Lessons* series. *The Top 50 Instant Bible Lessons for Elementary* includes the same types of resources for Sunday-school teachers as our preschool book: reproducible hand-outs, arts and crafts templates, puzzles, games, and step-by-step instructions. Ages five to ten years.

ISBN: 9781628624984

The RoseKidz Top 50 series continues with the *Top 50 Memory Verse Lessons*. Memory verses are vital to hiding God's Word in the heart and mind of every child. This book is packed with fun, interactive, creative, and engaging ways to get children excited about memorizing Scripture. The 50 verses are in an easy-to-learn format. Ages five to ten.

ISBN: 9781628625059

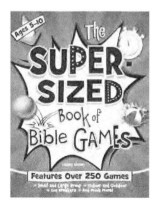

This *Super-Sized Book of Bible Games* is a giant, HUMONGOUS book packed with over 250 exciting games for every occasion. Each game has an overview, step-by-step instructions, supply list, Scripture connection, discussion questions, and a teachable moment connecting God's Word to the activity. Find exactly what you need with its quick and convenient index arranged by topic, type, and Scripture.

ISBN: 9781628625462